Stand as One
Spiritual Teachings
of Keetoowah

Awakening to the Original Truths

by

Crosslin Fields Smith

Dog Soldier Press
P.O. Box 1782
Ranchos de Taos
New Mexico 87557

First Edition October 2018
Second Edition March 2021

Library of Congress Control Number: 2021902278

Printing: Kindle Direct Publishing
Print ISBN: 978-1-7362743-5-4
Kindle ISBN: 978-1-7362743-6-1

Text editor: By his request and with the guidance of Crosslin Smith,
Dr. Clint Carroll edited the text for publication from transcripts of source
material provided by Marial Martyn, Ph.D.

Source material: Over eight years working with Crosslin Smith, Marial Martyn, Ph.D.
developed the source material from which this book has emerged.

Book cover concept: Crosslin Smith

Book interior and cover design: Ananda M. Sundari

Publication editor: Ananda M. Sundari

Back cover photo: Courtesy of the Cherokee Nation Communications
Department

This work is dedicated to all people,
in the spirit of unity and compassion.

Table of Contents

Coming to Know the Spirit:
My Life and Experiences

I was born November 27th, 1929, in what is known in history as the Great Depression of the 1930s. We weren't affected by the depression, because we knew how to survive. Like our ancestors before us, we survived through a lot more hardships than the 1930s. We raised our own food. We gathered things from the land, like varieties of edible plants, and we hunted game. In my early years, I retained what my mother and father and the other elders talked about. It would seem that everybody could retain stories like that, but not everyone did. The things that are going to appear in this book are based on my memory of what I heard when I was a child and when I was growing up.

I was given extra perceptions at birth, you might say spiritual gifts, to understand and interpret the meanings of what was said, including the rituals. Not only that, they say I was born a twin - that my brother died right after birth. I suppose it's the traditional way not to tell people about what happened. No one really told me that I was a twin. It was revealed to me in a strange way. One day my brother told somebody that I had a special gift and that I might be able to help them. He told the person that I was born a twin. This is the only time it was mentioned. That's how I came to know about it. In those times, if that knowledge was exposed to me early, in my untrained way, I may have misused the fact that there is a special gift in being a twin. So, it's for that reason they probably didn't tell me.

I would come to know in my mature years not only that I was born a twin, but also that I was born with a veil - a membrane cover over my face. And traditionally they do something with that membrane so that the power will stay with the child. I was also born a seventh child. These traits are what gave me spiritual character. I think those traits are respected universally by various factions and various tribes and peoples. The traits don't develop early on, even though you have a keen sense of perception and understanding of situations. It takes time and maturity for them to develop into something useful. And at that time, they are used only to assist life. And what I will discuss later as "the Spirit" is the highest concept in traditional healing, even though there are a lot of different elements that can stymie and block you from maintaining your spirit.

The overall dissatisfaction with our circumstances during the depression stirred something within me. I knew there had to be more to life; that life had got to be better. You look at the options around you. In that time, we had some revivals - various religious denominations that were traveling over the country. I'd hear them talk about something that is just out of reach, so to speak. Some spiritual elders would talk about this better thing. It was a most remote thing that they talked about. It was like a dream. In reality, we were so poor that I just had to say these things they are talking about are unattainable.

Out of the depth of my young thinking, I began to think about what I had heard the missionaries say about having a good character, and how the medicine men I had listened to must be talking about the same thing. But, I asked, how come they are so different from one another? In my young mind, I began to think, silently, is it true that there exists a Supreme Being? If so, I asked, "How come you don't show yourself? How come I am the way I am? How come we are nothing in the community, everybody looks down on us, everybody makes fun of us? We can't compete in school because of the un-modern conditions that we are living in. There has to be something better." Again, I asked the Creator, "If you exist, where does this kid find you? Where do you live? Along the river? In the canyon, or in the forest, or the mountains? Where are you? Can you show yourself? Then I will understand."

Then things happened to me that were phenomenal in nature. I captured wild animals without any real assistance. I picked up a rattlesnake and took it back to its den. I didn't know how I did it. It wasn't me that did it. On a normal basis, I would be just as frightened and as scared as anyone. But, the thing that I did, when I said "Why don't you show yourself?" - that is when he began to show himself to me through these events.

I would go on to do phenomenal things with the sacred in my life. Later in life, I began to have flashbacks, not an alarming type, but just looking back at what state of mind I was in when these things happened. For example, there was a flock of birds bathing in a pond on my way to school. At that moment, I couldn't describe it - in a way, I just felt free. I felt good. I had a good image of myself. I had pride. I was in communion with everything, and one of the birds came out of the water and sat on the edge. As I got closer, the rest of them took off. The one bird sat there, and I picked it up. Returning back to my conscious mind and body, I thought, "there is something wrong with this bird, it must be injured." At that moment, I was coming from the perspective of my physical body and mind, thinking that there was something wrong with the bird. But in my communion with the world as a free spirit, I know now there was nothing wrong with it.

There are three parts to every person. First, there is just Spirit, and second, our body and mind. If we put all three together, then the ability to do these kinds of things is made available. As I grew older and looked back, I learned what state of mind I was in. It would come and go. It would come in to play when I needed it. Most of the time I ignored it. I was separated from my spirit. I was coming from the perspective of my physical body. When you make decisions coming from your body, you are going to goof up. All three parts have their own sensations. The mind, the body, and the Spirit. They are like three different characters. You have to pull those three together to be a whole person. Now that kind of knowledge you don't learn in college or anything. To some degree it was a subconscious education. It developed as I grew older.

In the Keetoowah way, parents dedicate certain gifted children with blessings by performing rituals over them, or by separating the child from the rest and leaving them certain kinds of food at isolated places. These practices ensure that when these children grow up, they will be of some service to the people. It is a dedication by the elders and by other people. It is a dream come true from the forefathers of the past. In troubling times, for example, when our ancestors were removed from our homeland to our new location, they said, "We are having trouble at this moment. There is nothing that we can do with our power at this moment, but we pray that one day someone will be born into the spirit world. That they will carry the kind of power that we should have maintained, so that we wouldn't have these problems." It is like a prayer from the past that the spiritual truth of this world would be revealed. That is another aspect of what happened to me.

When I was young, I overheard my father (he didn't know that I was eavesdropping) tell an elder as I was walking away, "See that boy? He is going to be somebody. He is going to be real spiritually strong. He will help a lot of people in his time." They knew that. Spiritual things cannot be manipulated. Spiritual things cannot be structured. The highest educational institution in this world cannot teach spirituality unless they know what that Spirit is. That element is missing in Western medicine.

Thanks to the Creator, I have had a good life, even though I come from a very dysfunctional and poverty-stricken Indian family. However, these spiritual attributes that I have described have put me through a lot of things. Of my generation, I am one of the few individuals who went to school. I started my education at a boarding school. I made poor grades in high school. I graduated high school, but I had nothing that would be considered college material, as far as I knew. I worked in my hometown of Vian for two years before I served in the United States Army, where I eventually served in the Korean War. I got to be a Sergeant and was in charge of college graduate draftees. That sort of gave me a sense of confidence. As an order from the Captain, I taught personal hygiene and hand-to-hand combat to college graduates. Whatever I was instructed to do, I did. Little did I know, that was a college preparatory experience.

What helped me too was that when I went to enroll in the Army, there was a bunch of my buddies enrolling at the same time from Oklahoma. I belonged to them. We were a family, regardless of what family they came from in the state. Some of them came from prominent people, but we shared a common thing in war. We didn't care where that boy come from.

You relied on him, and he relied on you. You had a common objective, a common enemy in the North Korean army, and you became a family whether he was black, Indian, or whether he was the mayor's son or somebody like that. It was different. We treasured one another. When I went to college, that was also the way it was.

I spent fourteen months on the 38th parallel. The Chinese army had a small excursion against us. In the process, I lost fourteen of my best friends one morning in a daylight attack. The day before I had an uneasy feeling. Something was in the air. I didn't really know what. But in the evening I stayed with one-half of the platoon that would rest until midnight, and then we would relieve the ones that were on the frontline. We were to let them rest and go on guard until daylight. Because I was having that certain uneasy feeling, I did a prayer that my older people taught me to ask the invisible world to protect me while I slept. I slept with a rifle across my chest in a bunker. Then I went to sleep sitting there. When I woke up, something that had to be about three feet tall (because I was sitting down) started putting his hand on my shoulder and whispered in my ear, and said, "It's time for you to wake up. Your enemy is coming close."

I knew exactly what it was: The Chinese army was about to attack. So instead of relieving the half of the platoon on the frontline, I called on the field phone and said, "You stay put. We're going to join you. We're going to be one hundred percent alert." At about 12 o'clock midnight, the Chinese army - they always blew taps down in the valley - and right after that, they attacked. But we repelled the attack. The invisible little people that I asked to protect me had given me the information about my enemies. Many times I depended on those invisible ones. We were on Pork Chop Hill on the outpost - it happened to be on Thanksgiving Day, I think, because they brought us some fruit and things to eat. I was sitting next to a bunker and I guess we were real negligent, laying around the outpost, sunning ourselves, and eating fruit. Low and behold, I heard this buzzing sound - whenever there's a mortar coming in, before it hits you can hear that buzz. I heard that. I fell over in the trench and right where I was sitting that mortar round hit. I cheated death again, one more time.

After coming home from the war in 1951, I entered Northeastern State College in Tahlequah, Oklahoma. I went there on a lark, you know, fully aware that I was going to flunk out because I didn't have any academic support. My friends and I had a ball that first semester. I hardly opened a book. I just used my common knowledge. You would be surprised how much you got going for you when you're on the spot. A person doesn't really know what they have until they are tested. So, in that first semester, I averaged out a C. When I entered the second semester, I thought, "Okay, what would happen if I tried?" I settled down more, and I made the President's Honor Roll. Sort of unbelievable. The professors saw something they liked. I was really well-liked, although I realized that I could compromise that if I wasn't careful. It wasn't a problem with the institution, it was just hard for me to let go of the damage that was done back in my childhood days when we were discriminated against because we didn't have modern facilities. That hung on to me quite a bit. I kept to myself, avoiding these people that liked me - the faculty, the student body. Maybe it is good that I kind of held back. I might have gone to an egocentric place and really messed up. So, from then on until I got my degree, I acted just like anybody else.

But thinking back on making the Honor Roll: How the staff liked me, how the student body liked me - I realize that the Creator was there, even though I couldn't see him. I graduated in 1957 with a degree in Education. I got a job in Brigham City, Utah, in the middle of Mormon country. For about 25 years, I served my civil service in Utah and Arizona as a school counselor for the Bureau of Indian Affairs.

In the early 1960s, I was called back to the Cherokee Nation to help rehabilitate the tribe. Due to Oklahoma statehood in 1907, there was no tribal organization until the 1960s. Statehood had taken the tribal government out, and our tribal representatives were appointed by the United States President. W.W. Keeler was one of the presidentially-appointed chiefs that signed off on things. Keeler was also Chairman of Phillips Petroleum, and he had his own little tribal executive committee that he selected to coordinate the tribal rehabilitation. The people, in general, didn't know anything about what was going on. For that reason, he recruited me from Arizona, where I was working at the time, to come back and help start the Cherokee Nation. Keeler and the BIA area director in Tahlequah came out to interview me. They wanted a bilingual person because at that time the general population of the Cherokees didn't know anything about what the tribe was doing. The tribe had a $1.14 million lawsuit against the Federal Government for the land that was taken from them within the Cherokee Nation, as well as the land that was taken from them in the Oklahoma Territory.

When I was recruited to come back home to do reconstruction and build Cherokee Nation to get the general public of the Cherokee people involved, it became my job to hold community meetings in the 14-county area of the Cherokee Nation. That movement established the first elected group in the Cherokee Nation by communities that were known as "community representatives." Each community elected two people who would go to Cherokee Nation meetings to get information and come back and share it with the people. That program was really successful. They were accepted by the General Counsel and W. W. Keeler gave them voting rights to all the issues taking place in the Cherokee Nation. At that time, I was a very popular person. I'm still a popular person.

We developed Cherokee Nation from scratch into what it is now. We re-developed the Cherokee Nation nucleus - the political structure of the tribe. We got the Cherokee population interested and active. All during this time, I just worked and was happy. I had a pretty good job. I had a few problems here and there, but all in all I would come out of it. But then come the political factors.

When we returned to holding our own tribal elections, a lot of people thought that I was interested in running as a candidate. They thought I had the motive to be Chief, that I was going to run, but in reality, I wasn't interested. There were other factions that came into existence. It was hard to convince people that I was only interested in the betterment of the whole tribe, that I didn't have any ulterior motives, and that I was working for the public good. They seemed to lose sight of that. While I didn't have any ulterior motives, I was subject to being socially degraded and isolated in my job. I was given jobs where I wouldn't have contact with the public, and so on. For that reason, I decided things were not going good. A little flier came across my desk from Washington, D.C. about Indian Law Prep School. I penciled out the application and sent it in. A few days later, I got word I was accepted. I began law prep school at the University of New

Mexico, and I saw this as my way out of the dilemma back home. I passed my law entrance test. I was then accepted at Tulsa Law School.

Like before at Northeastern College, I was not really devoted. I thought, "Maybe my future is in the spiritual world, not in law." Yes, spiritual law, but not the Western law. Nonetheless, I went for the first semester. Things started getting serious, but my family was still living in Tahlequah. If I wanted to continue, I would have had to get an apartment somewhere close to school, and I would have had to sell out and bring my family with me, so they could be with me right there. Some of my classmates were getting divorced and marrying a good stenographer. That was how they were going to get through law school. I didn't see a divorce in my life. I wanted to keep my family. At that point, maybe it was a blessing for me that my family didn't want to give up their home in Tahlequah and move. I thought, "Is working within the four-walled office really worth it just to be an attorney?" I always had claustrophobia with the dominant Western culture anyways. I thought even though I may have been a good attorney, I would have been isolated. It would be hard for me to conform to the code of ethics that the attorneys have. It is really a regimented program in the Western world. So, at that point, I decided I would drop out of law school, but that I could come back to it if I wanted to. When I dropped out, I came back and reinstated with civil service to finish out my 30-year tenure.

The BIA gave me a job at Carter Seminary in Ardmore, Oklahoma as a school counselor. Then I came back home and stayed in the Bureau for a while, until one day they said the Tribe wanted me back. They proposed that I do a what was called an Inter-Personnel Liaison contract - an officer on loan from the government to the Cherokee Nation. I still was a federal employee working for the government. At that time, W.W. Keeler said, "I want you to be something like a chaplain for the Cherokee Nation. They won't accept the chaplain title, so we'll give you the title of Tribal Resources Officer, the first advisor to the chief and council." I functioned in that capacity until I retired in 1978.

I was a medicine man, like a chaplain, to the Cherokee Nation. W.W. Keeler and Ross Swimmer - they were very knowledgeable about spirituality. If there was any conflict in any department of the Cherokee Nation, they advised me to walk through that department without talking to anybody. That's extreme understanding of the spirituality by those people. At that time, we didn't have any problems. Today, the general council and the representatives of the Cherokee Nation are always split and divided and quarreling with one another.[1] The absence of that spirituality is a major problem in the Cherokee Nation or anywhere else as far as that goes. During those times, I provided our Principal Chiefs with sacred water treatment rituals, including W.W. Keeler, Ross Swimmer, Wilma Mankiller, and now Bill John Baker. I even treated Ross Swimmer for his lymphatic cancer.

Things started picking up in the spiritual world when I came back home the second time. People began to ask me for services. At that time, I was about 45 years old. My father was a medicine man. My grandfather was a medicine man. I come from a family of spiritual people. They kind of thought, "Well, he should have inherited something. Maybe he knows some of the things that his father knew." And so, they started coming. At first, I would kind of refrain from getting deeply involved in their situation. Mostly, I would give them advice, like a consultant. I would consult with them. It grew from there until it really mushroomed.

The basic fundamentals of healing are the things you must ask yourself. How do you teach image? How do you teach a value? How do you get across to a person in the process of being healed that you must be in complete communion with yourself, mind, body, and soul, and in communion with the world? It is a very key concept of healing that you can't be helped if you got a bunch of chips on your shoulders or if you got the wrong attitude, the wrong emotions. Those are a hindrance to the healing arts. That will block you from getting help. People come, and I must counsel them on what they have to straighten up in their life or what they have to do away with in their life in order to come through and be healed and be helped - whether it is a court session or a marriage problem, or an abuse of some kind.

Once they start listening, then the question becomes, "How do I im-

---

[1] Although this statement was true at the time of writing, the situation has since improved to be more harmonious among members of the tribal council.

plant an image in a person who doesn't have any good images of himself? How do I implant a value in this person that they don't understand at this time? How can I ever convince them to be in communion with their own self?" And so, the image that a person has of herself has to be the best image possible. That positive self-image can produce pride. A true pride, not a false pride.

You have to have a rapport. If you don't have it, you have to get trust, confidence, all those things that go to make a rapport between you and your client. You never do anything unless you are confident of that. But you have to have a relation, a spiritual relation between the two of you. Then you begin to take out the things that shouldn't be in that person's mind and replace them with what is supposed to be there.

Some people who don't fully understand how the medicine works look at that with a negative attitude because they don't know spirituality. Those people can even come from the various ceremonial grounds we have. So, every day you build somewhat of a confrontation to people who don't really know what they're doing. But then again, I don't entertain that. I disregard the confrontation. I cope with it, and continue to depend on the strength and resources of the spirit world.

Chapter 1

The Spirit

Keetoowah teachings stress that when we come into this world, we are born with an inherent gift of Spirit that is given to us by the Creator. The acknowledgment of this gift and the acknowledgement of our inseparable connection with the Creator provide the foundation from which all spirituality is based. This spirit can be used to become one with all creation - that of yesterday, today, and tomorrow. Some people have a hard time understanding what that really means.

When we speak of yesterday, we have in mind all people, all the parts of creation that ever were. The bodies of this creation come to an end by death, but the Spirit never dies. Honoring the spirits of the past, no matter where they may be, is the highest requirement of the Keetoowah faith. In the same manner, honoring the present spirits of all creation - all the people of today, regardless of race, creed or color - is another requirement. If you can accomplish this, you will have the most favorable outlook on life, supported by the Creator. One must also do this with all the life that will be - the entire human race of tomorrow. This spans across all religious teachings, and is extended to include the Christian belief of the second coming of the Son of God, or Jesus Christ.

The highest objective in the Keetoowah faith is to be chosen by the Creator to continue life even after this earth is gone. This means that we believe in life after death, but not only as regards the body. This includes life after this earth, and our faith acknowledges the ones that may replenish another earth, if there is to be one.

The best words I can think of to explain these fundamental teachings are:

A complete, comprehensive respect
for life and creation that has no end.

The highest objective in healing is to maintain the Spirit, and not let negative things get in the way. One must keep the Spirit above and beyond everything else. We must attach everything to that spirit that lives in us. And all meditation and all prayers should be directed to that spirit. It requires a good attitude. It requires pride. This will give you a well-rounded, successful personality.

You have to be a spiritual person to be able to heal others. And to be a spiritual person, you have to know that the Spirit is within you, that it was given to you when you were born. The healing abilities come only to those who have learned to harness up the Spirit. It's like you disconnect from everything. You blank everything out, even to a point of dematerializing all except the Spirit. It takes a very, very deliberate sense of dedication - a sense of worthiness. What you are trying to do is present a pure spirit - not what you look like, not what you wear; not how mean you can look or how good you can look. You must have no ulterior motives.

Further, it is not the individual who takes the credit for healing others. All credit is given to the Spirit. So, as long as you keep yourself out of it, then you are okay; but just as soon as you put your ego into play, or let it go to your head, then you have lost it. It is a gradual thing. I first knew it when I was very young, but I didn't understand it. Western medicine and the human personality distort the meaning of these original healing concepts. They have their own interpretations of them, which lose sight of the sense of pride and the communion with the Spirit that is necessary.

The Sacred Water Ritual

The sacred water treatment ritual that we do with our people is the blessing of all blessings. It has a connection back to who we are and where we came from. It has never been recorded in any form until now - it's gotten away from publicity, miraculously, all these years. I describe it here because I believe it's time for all to know. I believe the spiritual knowledge that I describe in this book is for all humanity. We can no longer afford to support separation among peoples, separation within the self, or separation from our past and the future. I believe that today we must honor and nurture our oneness with all humanity.

In the water treatment ritual, I tell my clients that we need to have the best attitude we can muster up and to be proud of ourselves. In that moment, we need not to think about anything else. Not even our physical bodies. We have to stay with the Spirit and not let anything disrupt that spiritual state of mind, because that spirit is something that goes beyond everything else - beyond boundaries. It is related to every creation that ever was, every creation present today, and every creation that will be in the future. So, in performing the ritual, we have to retain our spirit and not let anything dampen that - your own adversity, or whatever it may be, just blank it out. Don't even think about your race or your identity - just know that there's a spirit in your body that was given to you by the Creator.

To perform the ritual, I prepare a trough or a bowl of well water and stand facing east with the person I am performing the ritual for. I hold a stick from the spicewood bush, and I make what I call "projections" in the water with the stick. The projections are slight motions in various directions. The first projections honor all the people of the world, according to their original symbolic colors. One represents all the brown people, the next projection represents the blue people, followed by the yellow people, and finally the black people. I make circle in the water that represents the earth on which we all live. I make a square to represent the divine square, and project into the universe to ask for blessings and protection from all negative forces. I do the same projection to the center of the earth, and another projection perpendicular to the earth's covering. Finally, I make a projection to every star in the universe, so that there is a true reflection of us in this place, at this moment. This is the process that makes this water holy. It is holy water now.

I ask the person to say their name out loud, and then I recite a prayer for that person. After I have prayed and asked the Creator for protection and blessings, I sing our original thanksgiving song. I then instruct the person to take a small amount of the holy water in their cupped hands and throw it behind them, over their head. They are to do this twelve times. After that, I instruct them to wash their face in the water, again repeating this twelve times. When they've finished washing their face, I then tell them to turn away from the water in a counter-clockwise direction before they return inside my house ahead of me.

That ritual goes beyond history. It goes back to the beginning, and it remains unchanged today. As I said before, it's a blessing of all blessings - it covers everything. Boys who are going to war are given that treatment. Many people who are supposedly terminally ill ask for last rites with that, knowing that they are on their way. There have also been people with a terminally-ill diagnosis that have turned it around with this treatment, and they have gotten well.

The water ritual encompasses all twelve Keetoowah spiritual acknowledgements. They are concepts that acknowledge the sacredness of all life, and all that we depend on for health and well-being.

Number one is the Spirit that is within you.

The second one is the Father Spirit from which your spirit came.

The third concept is for those two spirits coming together. You might call it a reunification. You must not have any greed, selfishness, or egocentric thoughts in order for that reunification to take place. Any negative element can interrupt that reunification.

The fourth one is the air we breathe. It is this air that connects us to all living beings. When we honor the air, we are in communion with life. Air is the breath of life and when in communion with the Spirit, air is a source of healing. It is medicine that can heal.

The fifth one is the water that we are made up of. We are also connected to creation by water, as it sustains life and is a cleansing agent.

The sixth one is the earth. The earth is our place of origination, and is the source of healing energy. The earth gives us food, shelter, and clothes. The soil itself can be the strongest of medicines.

The seventh is the holy light - the eternal flame, or fire. We must honor that fire, for our warm bodies represent the heat of that fire. The eternal flame is in the spirit of every person.

Number eight is the Brown Spirit, honoring the first created brown-skinned human from North America.

The ninth one is the Blue Spirit, honoring those people commonly known as white from the European countries. However, you can't identify a race with the color white because that color belongs only to the Creator. The color white is synonymous with the eternal flame.

The tenth one is the Yellow Spirit, honoring the yellow race of people, which covers the people from the Asian countries.

The eleventh is the Black Spirit, honoring those peoples from the African continent.

The twelfth is the eternal energy that is formed after the reunification mentioned above - the total, comprehensive, eternal nature of spirituality that one earns by honoring the reunification of the spirits.

My grandfather, Redbird, used to talk about the Keetoowah faith as one that is larger than anything that you can imagine. A faith that is for all mankind. One that is used to render services to others; to uplift life. This means you can't have any prejudice. All the negative feelings have got to go, all the hate and false pride. You have to get to the core of life. It takes intellect to be able to broaden that to a worldwide, or even universal level. It's that big. The idea that we are just little specs way down here-that gives you humbleness. So, the basis of this healing is humbleness. It is an internal development, and no one can teach you except the Spirit, if you know how to commune with it.

I used to ask to see the Creator's face. And I did, after I was mature - or at least I thought I was mature. To explain how the Creator came to me, I have to tell you a story. During the 1960s, the state of Oklahoma had the biggest manhunt in history for an Indian boy that was alleged to have abused and killed three Girl Scouts. The story is not often told outside this area, but we here remember it well. In short, someone close to me was the medicine man for that boy, who was innocent. Phenomenal things happened in that episode. Hundreds of lawmen and volunteers were in search of the boy. At one point, they saw him walk into a cave. They surrounded the cave, and when they walked in to get him, a white dove flew out. The boy wasn't in there. When they hired famous track dogs from the east, both the dogs died.

They were going to apprehend the medicine man for harboring and abetting a fugitive. That is when I come into play. I did what I could do spiritually and politically. I found an attorney, and they overturned those charges against him. No law enforcement would go pick him up, even when they had a warrant out for his arrest. I went and picked him up and brought him in to the station to process him. When the case was thrown out of court, I felt good. Everything was going to be OK. I was directed by the Spirit to fix that and to heal that problem. I thought all was well, but the medicine man couldn't get over how I had helped him - that I would be there to love and protect him forever. His ego wanted the credit for everything, and it got the best of him.

He turned on me.

At that point, I again silently visited my creator, and I said, "You know how many times have I asked to see you. It looks like now that I am willing to give up my spiritual practice and give it back to you if this is what happens. I don't want to be any part of it anymore. I am going to quit. Then the Creator put me out of commission. I couldn't move, although I wasn't in pain. I stared into a blank space. In a few moments, I saw myself standing over there in the air and there I was - immobile. Then a small light came. It mushroomed into a big soft white light and inside that light stood the Creator. I saw him. I had asked for that all my life, and there he was.

He put me through many phenomenal things. He carried me. In the process, there were no words exchanged. It was just vibration. He released things to me. He asked me questions. He was my teacher, and still is. He is the one that heals people as long as I am in my proper perspective in my own heart.

Afterward, I came to realize what knowledge he had released to me, as if to say, "I have given you my spirit. I am in your body all the time. That

The door to Crosslin's healing room. Photo by Clint Carroll.

spirit is like an invisible child of mine in your body." At that point, I knew that that spirit is the strongest thing in everybody. Many people don't realize that God is in their body. He also showed me that he was the father of that spirit, as if to say, "Learn to unite your spirit and my spirit. You shall have eternal energy - divine in nature - to assist you in your work. And you shall hold true that the air I have given you, that you breathe, is divine. And that the water I have given you is divine. And that the earth I gave you to live on is divine. And the brown grandfather that I created from dirt in the beginning, and the blue grandfather, and the yellow grandfather, and the black grandfather. Those are the original concepts of spirituality that I have given to everybody."

We are talking about an ancient spirituality that has been in existence since before Christ, but that is able to acknowledge other religious teachings. When you become one with the Spirit - mind, body, and soul - you become a well-rounded, whole creation. You send your spirit to connect with all those who have gone before you, whether they are in heaven or whether they are floating around on earth without a body. You make it right, spiritually. You make it right with everybody who is living today in this world. You make it right with everything that is to come, including the Son. Before Christ, when our ancestors did this, they had already become one with Christ even before he was born. That is the old concept. That's the spiritual concept.

When I learned these things, and I practiced them, I saw that the healing worked. I laid my hand on a person and made him well. Later, they came to me again to confirm that I had received what I was supposed to receive from the Creator.

After it was all over, an image appeared in the light and was inscribed into the wood grains of the door to my healing room. It showed the head and shoulders of the Father Spirit, with a robe extending to the floor. In his abdomen appeared the Son. And finally, the Mother Spirit above, her hair encompassing them both.

See - it's not me that heals people. The Spirits are my teachers. That's where the healing comes from.

In my work, there are three dimensions of healing that I must assess in every individual.

Pure oneness of the spirit is the strongest healing power, and highest gift there is for humankind. This is called the spiritual dimension, or the first dimension. It's not necessary to use plants if you have a full spiritual dimension.

Then we have a material dimension - those who are unable to comprehend the oneness of spirit and are unable to move beyond surface-level thinking and negativity. That is where plants and the substances within plants can be utilized to facilitate health and healing. Since people are influenced differently by different plants, you have to know what plants will do what. You have to know how to select the right ones. For that, you do a diagnosis, which is one of the hardest things to implant in some-

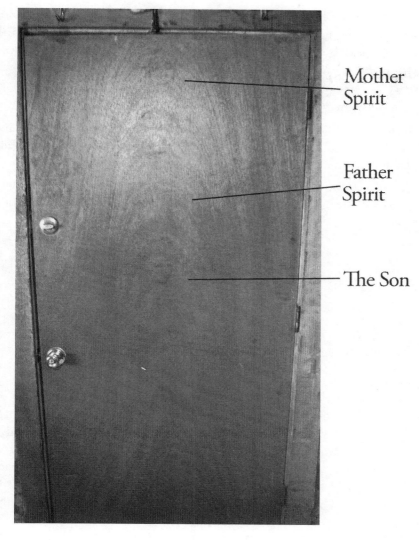

Mother
Spirit

Father
Spirit

The Son

The image inscribed on Crosslin's healing room door.
Above: the Mother Spirit.
Center: the Father Sprit with a robe extending to the floor.
Below: In the Father Spirit's abdomen, the Son.

one's mind. Just because somebody says a plant is for that purpose doesn't mean it's good for all people. It's only good for that which is compatible to the personality of the plant and the client. And that's a very hard concept to teach. They don't know how to match a person's personality with the personality of a plant. The plant has a spirit, as well as people. Those two have got to come together if it's going to do any good.

A man said to me once, "You gave me medicine that really worked, and I watched you get it. I went after it myself, prepared it, and it didn't do any good for me." So, there you have it.

The third, or lower, dimension of healing deals with extreme negativity. Unfortunately, many individuals live their lives in this type of existence. We just have to do what we can to try to help these people.

Healing Through the Spirit

What follows are a few stories that I want to tell that relate some experiences I have had in healing through the Spirit.

A truck driver somewhere down near Del Rio, Texas stopped at a truck stop, took a shower, and thought he'd have a cool drink - a beer. He walked to the bar, and there was a man sitting there. The man looked at the truck driver, and told him, "You need some help." The truck driver bought the man a beer, but he never did touch it. After a while, the truck driver looked back to the man at the bar, and he was gone. The truck driver, being part Cherokee, called Cherokee Nation and told them a little bit about what happened - that he supposed he needed some spiritual help. Someone at Cherokee Nation referred him to me. He drove his truck to my house, and when he walked in, he stepped back. His eyes got big. I said, "What's the matter? Come in, sit down." He said, "It was you that was in that bar." I have been told several times that I have appeared to people like that in hospitals and other places. And again, it may not be me that's doing it. The Creator could be using use another character who's more qualified, so to speak.

One of my clients at Claremore Hospital was scheduled to go to surgery for some kind of diabetes infection on her leg. She was scheduled to have her leg amputated when she called me. My advice to her was not to go into surgery that day. So, she refused to go to surgery, and I gave her medicine. She walked out of that hospital.

There was a person who was diagnosed with ovarian cancer. When she came to see me, my spiritual reading told me there was nothing wrong with her. I immediately requested for her to have a second opinion, go to another doctor. She followed my instructions. When she went to the second doctor, he gave her a clean bill of health. There was nothing wrong with her. One day I was invited to speak to about 30 or 40 doctors from a family medicine organization in Tulsa. I put the question to them, "What's wrong here? Why was there a diagnosis of cancer with the first doctor, and yet the second doctor said there was none?" Unfortunately, someone may have had dollar signs in their eyes. The first diagnosis that recommended chemotherapy, radiation, and even operation, would have led to about $70,000-80,000 in medical bills. My people don't have that kind of money. I'm not against the medical field, but there is something wrong with a diagnosis of that nature.

Another woman was diagnosed with ovarian cancer. The doctors said it was so far advanced, and nothing could be done. Somehow or another the woman's family found their way to come and see me. My diagnosis confirmed that she did have the cancer, but also discovered that there was a cure for it. I recommended that she take certain herbal teas mixed with a good alcohol, the alcohol only to be a vehicle for that herbal substance to go to all parts of the body, as well as the affected area. I recommended she take four doses. At the end of the third dose, I recommended that she go back to the same doctor and do a re-diagnosis of her situation. She did, and that doctor didn't find any cancer in that woman. He was amazed: "You're clear, you're clean. What in the world did you do?" She said, "I went to a medicine man and he gave me some tea and told me to take it." And the doctor wanted to know who I was and wanted to know if he could talk to me. "Well, that's up to him," she said. "I don't know if he'll talk to you or not." But she is well. She doesn't have cancer anymore.

~

In another case, a Native Alaskan woman was diagnosed with cancer and she went through radiation and chemo with no results. They still diagnosed her as having a cancer. They couldn't isolate what part of her body that was afflicted by cancer. And so, it would seem like they had run out of resources. So, they made a referral to the World Cancer Center in Tulsa. It just so happened that one of the students at the Center was studying with me at that time, Dr. Jody Noe. She happened to be the first to review the folder of this woman from Alaska. After scrutinizing the diagnosis and what they had done for her, she couldn't see any more that they could do except to repeat radiation and chemo. So, she called the doctors in and consulted with them. She noted that they would just be repeating the same treatment, so she requested to make a referral to me and the doctors agreed. They sent the woman down here with a hospital panel. I talked to her and explained what my diagnosis was.

In my diagnosis, I didn't see cancer. But I did see a negative energy that had been applied to her by her own people. Secondly, she had a very powerful spiritual concept within her personality that sullied the chemo and radiation that they gave her, and that's why it didn't show any help. So, what we had to do is to remove those negative factors from her personality and free her from all of this.

There were certain things we recommended. I proposed to perform rituals for her to exorcize the negative energy using water and herbal medicines. I said that if she was willing to go through with that, we could perform them that night. Otherwise, she was welcome to return to the hospital.

She said she would stay. In fact, she said, "If I had known this before, I would have come here before the Cancer Center." She was a good client and she did everything I asked her to do. We sent her back to the hospital. In a day or two, I got a call from Dr. Noe. She told me, "I just want you to know none of these doctors can find a sign of cancer in that woman. She's really happy and is on her way back to Alaska." So, what does that story entail? That negative factors afflicted a certain individual. The Western medical doctors don't have any means to handle this. In this case, it's like they were blindfolded.

⁓

Some years back there was a young girl who was having seizures. During these seizures, she would become several different people through her voice. Her grandmother was part Creek and Cherokee, and she could talk both languages. When the girl was having a spell, she would talk like her grandmother in the Creek language, but, on a normal basis, she didn't know how to speak Creek. Then while she was sleeping, somehow or other, something would use her body. She would be sleeping in one place, but people would see her walking around somewhere else. I guess you would say she was possessed. It took some time before my diagnosis could be confirmed. I had to build a rapport with her so that she felt welcomed, so that she'd feel OK to be with me. She was deathly scared to communicate with a man. That gave me some indication as to what had happened, but yet I couldn't tell her. I had to keep facilitating that conversation for her to say things.

By the time the congregation of her church found out that her parents were bringing her to a so-called medicine man, they were totally against it. In a telephone conversation, I could hear them praying against the devil in me. I know they weren't using their spirit, and I had to be confident that I was using the spirit that the Creator gave me and to stand by that come hell or high water. We reached a point where she was glad to come to the house, even though they had to steal her away from the congregation and come under the cover of darkness.

We got to where we would converse pretty good. I asked her, "When you go into these seizures, do you experience experience anything?" She said, "Yes, a man appears to me." I said, "Who is he?" She didn't want to say. She knew who it was. She said, "He calls himself Luke." That was my job - to find out who Luke was. I had a job to do, and we didn't need to go any further. I gave her some protection medication, in the form of tobacco and cedar, for her to use with water. I did my best to find out who this Luke was.

When she came back about the fourth time, I asked her, "Where did you get that name Luke?" She said it was in the Bible, chapter Luke. She said something happened during a Sunday school class. Somehow or other the Sunday school teacher was absent, so the minister had volunteered and they were studying the Golden Rule of what God had told Aaron and Elizabeth about her having a baby at 95 years old. The teacher was telling the kids that Aaron and Elizabeth did what God told them to do. He said, "When God tells you something, you must do it."

So, he used that Golden Rule to manipulate a beautiful twelve-year-old girl. He retained her and he told her, you must do what God told me for you to do. He molested her, and there was a split personality created. For the minister, he feared of that leaking out, and he recruited his deacons to put that girl down, satanically. They intended to do away with her, to shut her up for life. They were on their way to doing it. That's when I come in and started instructing her on the spirit and giving her four water blessings as an exorcism. The minister died, but I didn't kill him. It was his own doing, and the deacons soon left. That church is still there. The girl is a woman now, and has four kids.

Chapter 2

Origins

There is a Keetoowah story of creation that encompasses the origins of all humans on the planet. The way I heard the story is that when the Creator had completed creating the earth, he thought he should make a creation that would have stewardship over the earth and all other creations.

This creation would be the People.

To form this new creation, he used mud from the earth and a stick - they say he used a stick from the spicewood bush. He mixed his own tears, mucous, and saliva with the soil to make the mud, stirring it with the spicewood stick. Perhaps there might have been some blood mixed in there, similar to the substance that envelops a newborn baby. He had a brown powder, like the brown powder that comes from the center of certain rocks. They say he took that powder and stirred it into the mud. He gathered up a handful of that brown mud, and he formed a man. He liked the idea of that specimen. Then he gathered up another handful and formed a female. Then he took a blue-looking powder that is also found within the center of certain rocks. He put that in the mud and he formed a blue-looking, transparent skin person. You could see their veins that were blue in color. He created a male and a female. Then he added a yellow powder to the mud and he formed a yellow man and woman. Finally, he added a black powder to the mud and he formed a black man and woman. At that time, they were only lifeless figures.

He thought they would be the guardian creatures who will have stewardship over everything else. There was no implication in this about having dominion over one another. He didn't intend for someone to enslave another person. When he decided that's what he wanted, he took saliva and mucous from his nose, he spewed it on them, and they became living creatures. In the art of healing, we use this act of blowing with water and medicine to doctor our patients. The practice imitates the Creator at the point of human creation. It goes that far back. If you are with your spirit in the way you're supposed to be, you can heal by blowing your breath to imitate the breath of life.

When they became living people, he told them, "I have given you my spirit. You can be like me - you have my image. You are my children. Get along with one another, and teach your offspring this as a way of life." The Creator told them, "If you build me a temple, I will bring part of my holy light to that temple so you can have it to remind you to teach my laws."

All the people treated each other well at the beginning of this time, which we call the First World. They followed the Creator's law. But in time, the blue people became very adventuresome. I don't know whether that was a gift, or whether they generated it on their own, but they became industrious. They started building cities, and they made their own images to worship.

In my own thinking, it seems like they're talking about the cradle of civilization - somewhere near the Euphrates or Tigris River, where there was a very active volcanic mountain. It would glow in the night. And they believed that God lived in that volcano. Gradually, over a period of time, the yellow people drifted away from the main spiritual teachings, as well as the black people, as well as the blue people. They developed their own kingdoms and their own boundaries. They began to get paranoid at one another, and so they formed nations when there was supposed to be just one nation.

Then the god that lived in that mountain appeared and spoke to one of our ancestral elders. In Cherokee, we refer to this man as Sigil, which could be interpreted as Ezekiel. He called his name, and the man acted as if he didn't hear him. He kept doing what he was doing, and wouldn't pay attention. There was a second calling of his name, a little bit louder this time. Still yet, the elder didn't pay attention. He acted like he didn't hear him. And finally, in an abrupt tone, he called out his name, "Sigil!" Then the man paid attention.

The spiritual father spoke to him: "I'm very disappointed in the way that your brothers have made a mockery out of my laws. They have made a mockery of my holy light. They have made their own laws, the law of war. They are worshipping their own gods that they created. For that reason, I'm going to reveal to you a ritual. When you have completed it, there will be a curse upon the people who broke my law. Unknown disease, starvation, unmentioned weapons against one another. And you will have to leave this land."

This is how the ritual went, as directed by the Creator:

"Come to my sacred mountain. Find an evergreen tree that was struck by my sporadic light (lightning) and that has survived. Collect the green branchlets from that tree and return back home. Then take a sharp instrument and cut your forehead. Let blood stream down your face. When it reaches your beard, shave the beard off with the blood and mix the hair and the blood and the cedar together. Divide them up into three parts, and put those parts in three separate pouches. Take the first third and hang it underneath your skirt."

See, at that time and place, our men wore skirted garments.

"Then take the second third and go to the steps of the temple and cut it up into as many pieces as you can and scatter them to the four corners of the temple. Take the final third, and build a little fire in front of the temple. Put the third pouch in the fire, fan the smoke toward the temple. On the seventh day, remove the pouch from under your skirt and burn it, like the other part, in front of the temple. When you have completed this ritual, call upon the rest of the people."

At that point, they had multiplied to twelve nations, twelve tribes.

"Have them come together. Tell them I told you to move from this land. That you will travel toward the setting sun. You will become the world's traveler. You will go to every continent. That light they made a mockery out of in the temple, I will have retrieved it. When you are far away from here and still following me, I will give you that light."

That's how the Cherokees received the Eternal Flame. They say it came to them on this North American continent, through the meditation of seven holy men, or seven medicine men.

One of the stories that our people used to tell also takes place in this old land. There are three stars that come up early in the night to the east. Two stars are in line, vertically, and the one at the bottom, according to the seasons. Sometimes it's a little to the left in summer; in winter, it's a little bit to the right. They call those stars the three sons, or three brothers. Other people who study the stars call that the belt of Orion, or the Sleeping Giant.

This is the story they would tell:

A long time ago, when our people were beyond the waters to the east, in the valley of the Red Sea, there lived a family consisting of a father, a mother, and three boys. They had pretty much everything; they didn't need for a lot of things. They were truly pure. They were big and strong and spiritually right.

The oldest boy, he had a domineering personality. He would hardly settle for second place in any competition he entered into. If he didn't win, he was really disappointed. He didn't know how to cope with that. In modern times, you might say he had an ego problem. But he grew up, and he always had curiosity beyond bounds. He was always looking for something to do, something to conquer, places to go, just to say, "I've been there." That outlook might be good, or it might be bad, according to what he was venturing to do. But early on, he was really interested in what made the sky blue. And over the horizon it seemed like the sky meets the earth somewhere and he was very interested in that phenomena.

He told his father of his interest in seeing the place where the sky meets the earth. His father said, "Son, you've got some growing up to do. When you come of age, if you're still interested, we'll talk about it then. In the meantime, if you have that kind of project on your mind, you have to be true and strong. You have to keep in shape do the right things. Nevertheless, he continued to try to be "number one," even at the expense of overrunning somebody to get what he wanted.

Then he grew up, and he hadn't forgotten what his father said. He approached his father, who said, "That's a long trip for you to go on. You're going to have to get a lot of food together." I guess at that time, they dried everything to preserve it. Get your mother to help you so you have enough food for the trip. They were always very ritual-minded, using rituals for meditations and blessings. One of the best ritual treatments they did then, and that we still do today, was the water blessing. Water was one of the elements that was given to all life from the Creator.

So, when he was ready to go, on the morning he was to leave, he told his brother next to him - the middle brother - to come with him. They went to the edge of the water and they did a water ritual. He told his brother, "If, in a year's time, I'm not back, you are to come here and do this ritual. If blood should come forth from your nose, that's an indication I'm still alive but unable to come home." With that, the oldest boy left. On his journey, he came upon other nations. One of those places must have been somewhere in Africa, because there were black people there, and they accepted him as a visitor. Like all nations at that time, they still remembered how to treat one another - how to respect one another.

After a while, the boy traveled on, and he encountered other people, other nations. Somewhere along the way, he stayed all night by the sea-shore. The next morning, when he got up and was preparing his breakfast - probably boiling corn meal made from the parched corn and some dried meat - there was this creature, a person, who came out of the water. He was an old man, and he approached the boy and said, "I'm hungry this morning. I thought maybe you might give me some food or even some leftovers would do me."

Well, the boy - in his self-centered nature - hardly had time for anything else or other people. He told this old man, "No. What I have is for me, and I need this food for myself. I can't share any of it." The old man walked back toward the sea and disappeared. Little did that boy know, that was an angel.

He continued on his journey, and he met some wicked people. People who had turned to evil - cannibalism, witchcraft, sorcery. Anything you can think of in that black magic world, that's what they were doing. He met this old woman and she was practicing some kind of casting. He had enough spiritual power that he was able to get away, but not completely. He was mentally damaged to some degree. Then he continued on his journey, and finally came to this place where the sky and earth come together. There was an opening and closing phenomenon. When it would open, he would see beautiful land on the other side, and there was a small footbridge in between. He thought, "When it starts to open, I could dash through there and be on the other side when it closes."

So, when it started opening, he ran, only to find that the opening to the new world closed in front of him. When he turned back, the one from his old world closed behind him. When he looked around, he saw that there was little space on the sides of the bridge, and below the foot bridge was a volcanic substance.

He was caught between the two worlds.

A year had passed, and the second son went to water to perform the ritual like his brother had told him. When he completed his ritual, three drops of blood came from his nose into the water. They say this is why they call it the Red Sea. He went back and told his parents, "It has become my responsibility to go and find my brother and bring him home." So, his parents prepared him for his journey like they did the first son. The middle brother took the youngest brother to the water just as before, and told him, "If, in a year's time, I'm not back, do this ritual at the water. If blood comes from your nose, you will know that I'm alive, but that you need to come and get me."

The second son's personality was that of a follower. He worshipped his brother, and he always tried to be like him. He set out on his journey, and visited many countries. He came to the black nation and he said he was searching for his brother and that wished to bring him back home. The king told him, "Yes, your brother was here. We gave him the best blessings we could give him." The middle brother continued on, and camped at the same spot by the seashore where the older brother had stayed. In the morning, the same figure came out of the water and asked for food. Like his brother Like his brother before him, the middle brother turned the angel away. He came upon the wicked nations, and had a lot of trouble getting through them. Eventually, he made it past them, and he went the same way his older brother had gone to the place of the opening and closing between the worlds. Just like his brother, he thought he could dash to the other side.

He, too, was caught between the two worlds.

In a year's time, the youngest brother performed the water ritual, and he, too, saw blood come from his nose into the water. He told his parents, "I don't want to see what's over there. I just want my brothers back." The youngest son's personality was very kind and considerate. He really and truly had adopted the Creator's law to be one with everything. He was not aggressive. He was not a real competitor. He was easy to get along with. He had fully learned to be kind to all things, to all plants, animals, and people. His parents prepared him, and he went on the same journey.

He visited the black nation. While he was there visiting, he learned that the king of that nation was very ill, and had been for a length of time. The boy said, "I can cure the king. I can do that." The word got back to the king, and he ordered his royal guards to apprehend the boy. The guards brought him before the king, and the king said, "I hear you say that you can cure my ailments." And the boy said, "Yes, I can - provided that you have the right mind, that you have a oneness with all things at the moment I perform the ritual." So, he prepared some herbs and he built a small fire. He used the fire to heat his hands, and he laid them on the king, repeating certain prayers. The king got well.

The boy was then treated as a royal subject, as an honored guest. They were going to keep him forever, but he told the king, "I'm on a journey, out of love for my brothers, to bring them back home. They have gone to see what the other world is like. And they are being retained somewhere, somehow, and this is where I have to go." So the king let him go.

He camped all night where his brothers stayed, by the seashore. In the morning, the figure came out of the water, and before the old man could speak, the young man said, "Come and sit down. Share this breakfast with me." And they had their meal. It was a nice visit. When the boy was getting ready to depart, the old man pulled out a flute and he told the boy, "I'm going to give this to you. It will help you in a time of need. When your life is in danger, you play this tune. After you play it, name the animals who would like to help you out of the danger you are in." He played the tune for the boy. That tune is still used to this day in the water ritual to alleviate problems from afflicted people. It's one of our medicine songs.

The old man gave the boy the flute, and when the boy came to the wicked nation, he ran into a sorcerer woman. She tried to entice the youngest brother, but he refused. The sorcerer became very angry. She was going to turn him into anything and everything, and so he played that tune with the flute and then he named a wolf, a bear, and an eagle. They came out of that flute and they devoured this witch. At the end, the animals went back into the flute.

He finally got to the point between worlds where the other two had gone. In trying to save them, he too was caught between the two worlds.

Then a voice came from the other land - the voice of the Creator. He said, "You cannot come here by way of your strength and abilities. In order to come here, you have to come through the gates of death, provided you have lived the way I told you to live. I'm going to allow you to go back home with your youngest brother because he has qualified. He is a good person. He came only because he loved you, and for that reason, I'm going to allow him to take you back home. If you go back home and live the way you're supposed to, then when you die, you can come here."

They used to tell stories like this to teach, to capture the curiosity of the young people, and to get them to think. The answers weren't ready-made; they had to use their mind to decide who they are and what they are like. There are a lot of moral details in this story: Be careful who you follow, and be careful who you run with. You have to figure out whether they are genuine, true individuals, or whether they are fake people. If you follow a man and not the Creator, you're like the first boy. If follow somebody that you think is the one you want to be like, you'll be like the second boy. If you live according to our ancient rules, of being one with everything, then you'll be like the youngest son.

Chapter 3

Migrations

Our Keetoowah teachings say that a migration takes place at the end of the First World, or the end of our time in the old country. This migration comes in the form of a flood, and leads the people to another land. They say that this flood created new continents, including this North American continent.

The End of The First World

The story of the flood begins with a revelation that came to one of the elders. The revelation told him that the rain would come, and the land would be covered with water. It said to him, "Make a strong raft, like a cabin on a raft. Have it finished on this certain day." And this man did that. He was told to set adrift. He started pushing his raft into deeper water and there appeared a dog. This dog was sitting on the river bank and that dog spoke to him. "Take me with you," it said. "In the time when you are to lose your life, let me lose my life. Let me be the sacrifice." The fact that this dog spoke means there was one language for everybody and everything at that time - all creatures, not just humans.

So, the man and the dog set adrift, and the land was covered over by water. For many days they floated, and their food supply was running low. The dog spoke again: "Both of us are eating this food, and we're eventually going to starve to death. Do you know why I came along? I'm supposed to be the one to save your life. You need the food we have left so you can finish this journey." At that point, the man pushed the dog off the raft. The dog swam away. The man continues to float for many days. He had consumed almost all his food, and he was very weak - dehydrated and hungry. He was aroused from his near-death sleep by a scratching noise on the logs of the raft. He raised up, and there his dog was trying to crawl up on the raft. He thought, "Well, we might as well both die then." A lot of people would think about eating the dog, but nothing is said about that. He reached over and grabbed the dog by the back of his neck and pulled him onto the raft. When the man opened his hand, he saw there was mud. That dog had found land. And that dog led the man to the land. In our teachings, that story marks the beginning of the brown race's inhabitation of the North American continent.

When European explorers came over the Cumberland Gap, on the western slope, they came upon a stone carving of a dog, facing west, about ten feet tall. The historical society of Tennessee never did know the story behind that statue, and so it had no inscriptions. But our spiritual people can actually interpret the meaning of the dog facing west. We had come by this way, we had gone west. The statue was carved by the early inhabitants, because the dog helped man find land. God created that dog, and so they honored the dog by carving that statue.

Even the holy people from South America would venture to that spot, and they would leave an offering of some kind. They still remembered their origin and their heritage. Those who migrated to the southwest, the spiritual people, would journey back and give an offering to the statue. The same goes with the people who migrated to the north.

The European people, not knowing what that statue represented, knocked it over. The Onondaga Nation from the north in Canada came and re-erected it. But gradually, over the years, they still didn't know what it was, and they either shot it up or nature eroded it. Finally, the historical group of Tennessee started searching for the meaning of the statue. They called various tribes, including the Cherokee Nation, and they wanted to know if anybody knew anything about it. And the Cherokee Nation called me, and I said, "I know that story." I heard it many times when I was young. So, the next thing I know, I was invited to come up to Cookeville, Tennessee, and that's when I told them that story.

Looking back, I feel like maybe I didn't get it across to them, that when dealing with something sacred, they need to respect it. The same way we use our spirit to respect everything. With that story of the flood and the dog, the Cookeville Historical Society planned for a roadside attraction. Their intentions were not right. They didn't understand the spirituality of it, even though they were churchgoers. As a result, the people that were involved are all gone now. Today, they have reconstructed a column of rocks, and a part of that stone from the dog statue is sitting on top. They call it Standing Stone. Somebody recreated a carving of a dog, on a small scale, and the dog is sitting down and facing west. But due to the lack of understanding, people just don't know what they are looking at. The column of rocks with a piece of stone on top is at Monterey, ten miles east of Cookeville.

The Beginning of The Second World

At the beginning of what we refer to as the Second World, on this North American continent, life was good. There was a peaceful existence after the episode of the flood. For undetermined length of time, they lived the way they should, according to the rules that were given to them by the Creator. As they multiplied, factions began to be a major problem.

Conflict over leadership caused great divisions among the people. Very early on, my elders used to tell about three brothers who inherited the leadership of the tribe, to be the chief. Instead of sharing the position, they began to compete against one another. As a result of this conflict, one brother took those who would follow him and migrated to the northwest as far as Alaska. The other one took those who would followed him to the west, to the coastal areas. And the third one took those who would followed him to the southwest. And the same thing happened again. The conflict for leadership caused more factions. A number of times, they divided up again, calling themselves by different names. They say that's how the tribes came into existence on this continent. We can only guess the time frame of these events. It may go back to prehistoric times, according to how old this North American continent may be.

Time and again, the people were given a chance to return to the original rules. But their circumstances clouded what should have been a peaceful attitude toward all creation. The coming of the Europeans intensified their situation. They annihilated the first boat load that came. These may have been the Norsemen. They thought they had conquered the enemy, but then came more boats. This time they attacked them, but let one or two of them go. They hoped the men would go back to where they came from and discourage others from coming. Instead, even more boats came.

The people held a great council meeting of all the tribes. At that time, they had developed into the Mohawks, the Senecas, Modocks, Shawnees, Creek, and many others. They all came. They brought the peace wampum belt, a purely white beaded belt. It was laid on the table. Very quickly, they passed a unanimous war resolution against the European newcomers. They declared an all-out war to keep the Europeans from encroaching. They say there was a man that sat by the council door and watched without speaking to anyone. He would either nod his head or shake his head.

When they were about to adjourn the meeting, he got up and asked to speak to the council. He said, "It's very unfortunate that you passed a war resolution against humankind when you have those pure white belts laying there. What have you done? Those belts represent peaceful coexistence with all creation." At that point, the people thought the man was a messenger from God. They reconvened the meeting, and did away with the war resolution. They decided that they would also do away with the tomahawk, the principal war weapon. They added a bowl - a pipe - on top on the opposite side of the blade. With this instrument, they hoped that instead of raising the hatchet against humankind, they would smoke for a peaceful existence.

And yet, even with this peaceful intention, they made a mistake. The original practice for praying with tobacco is to offer it, not to smoke it. And the Creator's original design for the tobacco plant is to use it as medicine. When he created that plant, he made it into a medicine for anyone to use in order to get out from under depression, conflicts, and disease. No one can do a better job on that plant than the Creator. He speaks to people through that plant, almost like saying, "If you want my help through this plant, you will learn to offer it to the best things I have given you." Nowhere in this does it say to smoke it or burn it. The people made a mistake by smoking it in the pipe.

As an offering, the Creator originally instructed the people to offer it to the spirits and elements of creation. Offer it to your own spirit, which is a part of the Creator that he gave you when you were born. Offer it to the reunification of his spirit and the spirit that he gave you. Offer it to the air - he placed a spirit in the air. Offer it to the water - he has a spirit in the water. Offer it to the fire. Not necessarily a physical fire, but the warmth of your body represents the fire. Offer it to the earth. The earth provides you with everything. It gives you your food, it gives you your home, the garments you wear. Offer it to your brown grandfather, to your blue grandfather, to your yellow grandfather, and to your black grandfather. That's the original use of tobacco.

During the time when our ancestors had gotten away from the Creator's rules, they began to get sick. The time frame for this episode is unknown, but the holy people during that time were very discouraged, and they could only resort to the Creator for help and guidance. So, they went to a high point - a mountain top - and they fasted for four days. On the fourth night, they witnessed a storm brewing, with low clouds, rumbling thunder, and lightning. The clouds began to take on a continuous glow; a reflection of some kind of light in the clouds.

The voice of God came from that glow and said to them, "You have forgotten what I have told you. For, in my creation is medicine. If you honor all creation, good things will come to you. If you honor the plants and animals, you will find the cures to your diseases. Go back to the original rules, and I will give you a name. You will be known as *Keetoowah*. If you abide by my sacred laws and never lose sight of them, then you will be known as elder of all the tribes."

This event is interpreted as when we received the Golden Eternal Flame. We honor that by igniting our ceremonial fire in a special way, using only natural materials, along with prayers to be one with everything. We were told there is a spirit in this fire; that the fire represents the Creator.

Out of this knowledge, our ancestors created a wampum belt that depicts the design of the ceremonial stomp grounds and represents the seven clans. That's how the ceremonial grounds and the eternal flame of the Cherokees came into existence. Around the central sacred fire, there are seven arbors that represent the seven clans. The grounds are designed only to be entered through the west gate. At the fire, there is a log to the east, a log to the north, one to the west, and one to the south. They are there to honor all people - of the past, present, and future.

My great-grandfather, Pig Smith, was the head man of the spiritual group that moved out of North Carolina after the first encroachment of the European people. During that time, which was the early 1700s, the traditional Keetoowah had followed their original instructions - to move away from conflict and go toward the setting sun. But they also remembered what they were told by the Creator - that they would come to the edge of a great prairie, and that they were not to traverse it. He said, "If you do, you will lose your true God-given name, which is Keetoowah. You will just be another one of the members of the melting pot of the world." And so, by the early 1700s, Keetoowah people were already here in this territory that is now called Oklahoma. When they came to the edge of the great plains, they interpreted it as the great prairie that the Creator had spoken of. This is where they decided to settle.

The story of a great Keetoowah leader describes the way the ancestors first came to these lands. In Cherokee, his name was Ugewaleda. "He turned the page" is the best English interpretation that I can give from his original Cherokee name. He was the half-brother to Sequoyah, who invented the Cherokee syllabary. The story goes that back in the east, somewhere in Tennessee - maybe around Red Clay - when our people lived in that area, a certain party of men from the Osage tribe had ventured into the Cherokee territory. The Osage were from the area of what is now Missouri and Oklahoma. The Osage encountered a Cherokee hunting party and killed three Cherokee men.

The three Cherokees had been scalped.

Evidently, the Osage, knowing they had done something wrong, began to retreat as fast as they could, back to their home area. The leader of the Cherokee hunting party survived, and went to his chief to report what had happened. The chief called for one the most accomplished war leaders. To be a war leader, of course, was going against the Keetoowah original values of peace. But in those times, it was necessary to defend their people.

The one the chief called on was Ugewaleda. The chief told him, choose seven good warriors and pursue the Osage, but only to retrieve the scalps of our people.

They pursued the Osage, and the first area they traveled to was what we know now as Little Rock, Arkansas - along the river. A flood had deposited a pile of small pebbles, or little rocks. Ugewaleda told his party, "This place shall be called the place of the Little Rock," and to this day that place still carries that name. In Cherokee, it is *nvyo tsunsdigo*.

They then pursed the Osage to an area that we know now as Van Buren, Arkansas, a place where the Spaniards had mined gold and probably some diamonds. They had left an old fence, a railing fence. He told his party, "This place will be known as the place of the old fence." To this day, the name Fort Smith is called *uweti disoya*, or "a place of the old fence" in Cherokee.

They pursued the Osage across the Arkansas river into what later would be known as Owl Hoot Road in Nicut, Oklahoma. There they found a dead body. Ugewaleda told his party, "This place shall be known as the place where a man died." To this day, Nicut is known to the Cherokee as *yvwi tsvyohusv*, or "a place where a man died."

Then the pursuit came to the upper part of the swamp of the Arkansas River, which would be close to what is now Sallisaw, Oklahoma. The swamp was so thick they could hardly get through, but their perseverance was high in pursuit of the Osage. Ugewaleda told his party that the place will be known as "the place of the swamp." In Cherokee, Sallisaw, Oklahoma still carries that name: *saluya geyu'v*.

And they went down the Arkansas River, somewhere south of what we know as Vian, Oklahoma. The party witnessed a school of garfish - evidently, they were spawning. There was such a multitude of gars, and they weren't cautious of the men. Some of the party caught them by hand to make a meal out of them. So, Ugewaleda told his party that the place would be known as "the place of the gars." In our language, Vian still carries that name: *dahnugo'e*.

The pursuit went to the mouth of the Illinois River, which runs into the Arkansas River. They followed the Osage up the Illinois River up to what is now Fort Gibson. They saw a herd of spotted deer, which we interpret now as a herd of antelopes. This gives you some idea as to where and when the antelopes existed in this area. Ugewaleda told his party, "This place will be known as the place of the spotted deer." To this day, in the Cherokee language, Fort Gibson carries the name of "the place of the spotted deer," or *tsusqua gali.*

Then they went up the Illinois River, which branches off at Saline Creek and goes into the area of Spavinaw, Oklahoma. At that area, the party saw a lot of salt deposits along the river where the water had receded. They would scrape the salt off the rocks and collect it, because salt was something sacred to the people. He told his party this place will be known as "the place of salt." To this day, Spavinaw is called *amohi*, or salt town. At that point, Ugewaleda told his party, "Tonight, we fight." The pursuit had turned west toward the present-day towns of Oologah and Claremore, Oklahoma, which didn't exist then. They came up on the Osage, who were weary and sleeping. They attacked, and retrieved the three Cherokee scalps.

The Osage and Cherokees were at odds with one another for a long time because of those incidents. And W.W. Keeler brought the Osage Chief, Paul Pitts, to the traditional Keetoowah Chief, who was my father, Stokes Smith, and they finally made peace at these very ceremonial grounds down the road. From whatever time it was that this episode with Ugewaleda took place until 1958, they finally made peace with the Osage tribe.

On their return trip home, somewhere around Roland, Oklahoma, on the banks of the Arkansas River known as the red clay area, Ugewaleda told his party, "If you are a man who has completed the spiritual requirements, this is what you can do." He stepped to the edge of the bluff (to this day they say there is a footprint on that bluff), and he plunged his body into the river. This occurred sometime in the morning, and he didn't come up for a long time. The rest of the party thought their leader probably drowned, and thought they should continue home without him.

At about noon, Ugewaleda popped out of the water on the opposite bank and let out a war whoop.

The people who I heard this story from said that when he dove into the water, he transformed into a spider and crossed the river. When he reached the other side, he turned back into himself. I told this story because we have some characters in our history, like Sequoyah's half-brother

Ugewaleda, who was extremely spiritual and was capable of performing these things. He also gave us a heritage of the names of the places he traveled in pursuit of the Osages.

There are other stories they told that are meant to teach the people important lessons. One story is about three boys and a large serpent, a large snake. The snake had come to a ceremonial ground and it was so big it made a circle around the grounds. He opened his mouth, and there was a lot of pretty things in that snake's mouth. You might imagine neon signs, advertisement lights and things. It was beautiful. People were attracted to that. They began to go closer to where they entered that beautiful snake's mouth. All except three little boys, who had hidden themselves. They weren't attracted to the snake, but the snake had captured all the people.

Then an angel in the form of an old man that came to the three boys and said, "Why are you so scared and why are you crying? Why are you hiding?" They pointed to the white snake and said, "That snake has swallowed all our people." The angel tried to console them, and then he produced a bow with three arrows.

He told the oldest one to notch the arrow and shoot at the seventh diamond of the snake. The boy shot, but the arrow fell short, which meant that he would be a leader, but he would fall short in trying to save the people. Not necessarily from the snake, or whatever the snake represented, but from something unknown.

The angel asked the second boy to notch his arrow and shoot at the seventh diamond of the snake. The boy shot, and the arrow went past the first one, but fell short of its mark.

Then he asked the third boy to notch an arrow and shoot. He shot, and it fell short but ricocheted and hit the snake on the seventh diamond. That caused the snake indigestion, and he opened his mouth and all the people ran out.

They used to think that Redbird Smith, my grandfather, represented the first boy; that Redbird's second son, Sam Smith, represented the second boy; and that my father, Stokes Smith, represented the youngest boy, the third boy. They thought that my father's work would ricochet and reveal the truth of the Original Law, which should free a lot of people.

They had a subordinate interpretation of the snake, which isn't really important to me, but since they interpreted it that way, I'll go ahead and say it. They said the serpent represented the white man. The multicolored beautiful mouth represented all the different places one shouldn't go. That's the way they told those things, the best I can remember.

Another story depicts children playing at the seashore. The kids find a tortoise and they climb on its back to ride it. Their parents and others tell them, "Don't do that. Get off of it. That turtle is going to walk off into deep water. You'll be in danger." The kids say to themselves, "Oh, we'll get off soon." But then the tide shifts, and they are caught in the water and they can't seem to get off the turtle. An angel appears and turns the tide back for them to get off. There again, in the form of an angel, the old ones emphasized oneness with the spirits of creation as a concept to get past dangers. Time and again, the old ones reverted back to those original teachings.

They told this story to encourage kids to stay out of danger. To keep away from people that do their own thing, without listening to their elders. These teachings help the younger people to get straight. They used to orate these lessons to the whole congregation at the ceremonial grounds. That's what the grounds were for. To come and listen to the old one's lecture was just like a church meeting. Anymore it's just a fanfare - a place to go hear somebody beating on a drum and dancing around. They have forgotten what it means. They have forgotten the original teachings, and instead have misinterpreted certain stories that lead them down the wrong path.

One example of this misinterpretation is a story from the late 1700s, when the Spaniards were still in this country, but they were being forced out by the Americans. They were retreating back to Mexico when the Keetoowah people were already here. At one point, the Spaniards met with the Keetoowah council somewhere around Tallahassee, Oklahoma - north of Muskogee. The captain, whoever he was, told them, "I have to leave, but I'm coming back. When I come back, don't think of me as a thief in the night. Don't retaliate, be neutral. My military will use what little territory you have to get rid of these people that have come into this country. And when I come back, the blood will be as high as the horses bit. I'll come in like a broom. I'll sweep the country clean."

This captain that was speaking to our people around Tallahassee, Oklahoma was playing like he was Cortés, who had managed to deceive the Aztecs by playing God. Everything this captain said was taken out of the Bible. "The blood as high as the horse's bit" is right out of the Bible. "The thief out of the night" is also right out of the Bible. At that point, our people had forgotten a lot about who they were and what they were supposed to be following. Some of them took what the Spanish captain said to heart. They actually thought Mexico was going come back and take control the country again. Some of the ceremonial activities they were performing were centered on the fact that that was going to happen.

Unfortunately, to this day, there are still some factional group leaders who tell that story like it is going to happen. As long as there are still a few people who have the original state of mind about spirituality, they can still pull through. But when that's all gone and everything is contaminated, everybody is going to be fighting with each other.

If that happens, we're looking at termination.

Chapter 4

Renewal

Years ago, when the holy people of the Keetoowah Society realized that there was illness and corruption among the people, that many were mistreating one another and using medicine to manipulate when it was originally designed to support life, they came together to fast without food or water for seven days. They did this so that they may be enlightened by a vision from the Creator.

The location of this fast by the seven holy men is located near Tenkiller Dam, in Oklahoma. At that place, there were large flat rocks in a circle, which created somewhat of an amphitheater design. The holy men camped there for their vision quest. They had laid out a little water jug with a gourd dipper.

On the seventh night, as their fast was about to be completed, one of them woke up. He had an extreme thirst for water. He got up, and since it was past midnight, he thought it would be ok to take water into his system. And so, he went to the little water container with the gourd dipper, only to find that there was no water in the container. The water had come out of the container and there was a narrow strip of water to the east as far as the eye could see. So, he went back to rest until morning time. In the morning, when everybody woke up, they went to get a drink. The water was back in the container, as if nothing had happened. They realized that this was the vision they had sought. They agreed to come back together at another time to discuss the meaning of this vision.

There are no oral reports about their coming back together. If they did come back together, it's unknown. Some of the people interpret that vision as everything that the Indians ever owned will be taken away, including the land and resources. This interpretation is based on the gradual diminishing of resources that the Keetoowah people have witnessed. But, the vision is also interpreted to say that if the people keep with the objectives that the Creator has given them, then they will regain everything they ever owned. This is the interpretation of the water being emptied

John Redbird Smith standing with wampum belts.
Photographer unknown. Photograph provided courtesy of Paul W. Eichling.

and projected to the east as far as the eye could see. If they would live by the objectives that the Creator gave them, those who are yet unborn will come out of a deep deprivation and have everything they ever wanted.

This vision points to the fundamental principle of the Keetoowahs:
To be one with all creation, before, now, and tomorrow.
We could say this principle is to

Stand as One.

There are many sayings one could use from my ancestors to get this point across. One of those sayings is, "If you want to achieve success in whatever you set out to do, you have to start as though you are hand-in-hand with all of creation." That phrase comes from the teachings of an ancient belt, one of the sacred belts - the wampum belts. It's a belt that's about a hand-breadth wide and six feet long.

White Road Wampum Belt

At the bottom, on the purple background there are stick figures holding hands. That means you must walk hand-in-hand with your fellow man. There's a white strip with dark beads on each side. Supposedly, that's the narrow white righteous road. The only way you can be on that road is to be hand-in-hand with all creation.

The teaching is to hold out your hand to that dark side of life for anyone that wants to grab a hold. Help them, and teach them how to travel on that white road. For, in the ancient meditations they say that even though you can't see the Creator, he's got a hand out. You are to have an open hand, an open heart, to anyone that you can help - and not just for people who share your identity or race, but for all people. There's a little white square up on top of that belt. It's a sacred square that represents heaven. If you have done your best to stay on that white road, when you die, you get to go there in the afterlife. And if you have followed the original sacred law throughout your lifetime, you may go to the seventh dimension, which is the highest dimension of heaven after death. I don't know how old those belts are, but I would say that Indians knew about heaven way before any Christians did.

At some point in history, the United States government requested that they have an addition made to this belt showing the letters AM beside the stick figures. The letters signify America, and were considered a symbol of an alliance between the United States government and the Keetoowahs.

A fallacy that people often make lies in the manmade concept that these teachings are just for Indians, or Cherokees. Because of that concept, a lot of our people isolate themselves. They forget that the teaching says to hold out your hand to anyone, regardless of race, creed, or color. Our leaders at the ceremonial grounds are further restricting people to adopt an extreme, conservative mindset. Little do they know that they are preventing other people from sharing in this great thing.

Pure White Wampum Belt

As far as the other belts go, the most sacred one they had was the pure white belt. The original was made of pure pearls - they say the belts were originally made of pearls. That pure white belt represents oneness with all creation.

The Cherokees always said that your mind should be as white and as pure as this belt. It explains the concept of oneness, which is one of the objectives of the Keetoowah Society. They say that long ago, each tribe had a white belt like that. And even before the Indian tribes came into existence, a white belt was kept by the four peoples of the world: the black people, the blue people, the yellow people, and the brown people. Gradually, those belts disappeared. The few that remain are now mostly seen in museums.

Father, Son and
Holy Ghost Wampum Belt

The third most important of the sacred wampum belts is also white, but has three small squares outlined at the bottom, middle, and top of the belt. Those squares are divine squares, which could be interpreted as the domains of the father, mother, and child spirits. Some people refer to them as the Father, the Son, and the Holy Ghost. Those are the three most important belts in my interpretation.

Tomahawk Peace Pipe
Wampum Belt

The other belts have to do mostly with political history. I mentioned before the belt that depicts the tomahawk as a peace pipe.

Seven Clan Wampum Belt

There is also a smaller belt that represents the seven clans. Seven buckskin bars divide the wampum beads, representing the matrilineal clans: the wolf, the bear, the long hair, the paint, the bird, the deer, and the savannah. Our people were smart enough to say that this belt represents the "smallest law," or the "little law." By that, we mean not to take the place of the Creator's sacred law in the design of the ceremonial grounds that they developed.

Eternal Fire Wampum Belt

There is also a belt that represents the eternal fire. The design on the belt has the four directions, like an emblem, an ancient Cherokee cross. At the center of that cross, there is a dark square that represents the eternal flame. I give a lot of credit to the ones that developed these belts. They made them because they thought their people would become weak of mind and forgetful. So, they created these belts so that they could have something in the way of visual aids for teaching the younger people.

Keetoowah Medicine Pouch

To this day, there is one missing relic of the Keetoowah Society. It is a medicine pouch, about eight by eight inches' square. It is probably made from some kind of animal skin, and has fringes on the sides. On the upper right-hand corner of the pouch, there is a depiction of a new moon with a star in its cradle, known as the star of David. It forms a triangle from the tips of the moon to the star. At the lower left-hand corner of the pouch, there's a hand with the forefinger pointing to that star and crescent on the upper right hand corner. At the bottom of that pouch there is a hieroglyphic form of writing, similar to Sequoyah's syllabary.

Some say Sequoyah used and refined these old hieroglyphics to invent the Cherokee syllabary. They say the interpretation of those hieroglyphics is: "I am Israel, and Israel is mine. So be it."

These sacred relics impart valuable teachings that have been handed down to us by the Creator. The Keetoowahs have always known that humankind has a responsibility of stewardship over the earth. This is expressed in the stick figure wampum as a oneness with everything, but it is also taught through the story of when the Creator made the first humans out of dirt. Dirt, or soil, is one of the twelve sacred elements given to humankind. Through this knowledge, we honor the earth, because we get literally everything from the earth, all our food, our shelter, our clothing.

The Original Rule was to take from the earth only that which you need, and no more.

If you take something, leave an offering somehow, whether it is through meditation or otherwise. We were told that when you travel through the woods, you try to leave no marks that you've been there. And again, holding out your hand to other beings as the Creator instructed is a way of imparting a blessing on what you have received from the earth.

We should never contaminate a special gift from the Creator like the soil. If we were to enact a true stewardship responsibility for the earth, we wouldn't have the problems we are having today. Humans created the atomic bomb, the hydrogen bomb. We didn't know how to handle the storage of the waste this produces, and we still don't. We created something we don't know how to handle. They think they can contain it, but in time, the elements in the earth will corrode that and release it and much of our land will be contaminated, along with our food and water supplies. This is what brings the end of the earth in time. Today we have to ask if we are going to continue this, or if we are going to go back to the original teachings.

My grandfather, Redbird Smith, once said, "Our pride in our ancestral heritage is our great incentive for handing something worthwhile to our posterity. It is this pride in ancestry that makes men strong and loyal for their principle in life." His remark about ancestral heritage is an important one. This perspective was handed down to Redbird from his father, and his father before him - they were all holy and spiritual people. We have to remind our people time and again about these things in order to guide them toward a good way of life.

The old ones described the Tree of Life as something to be cared for, as a way of instilling this stewardship ethic. They said that's how you respect the Spiritual Father, by taking care of the Tree of Life. Prune all the dead elements from it, from the bottom to the top. The Spiritual Mother is honored in the same manner. And the third God, the Child God, you respect him in the same manner. Of course, the true Tree of Life is your body. The main thing that we honor is in our bodies all the time. Our ultimate goal should be to become one with your own spirit, and let that spirit communicate to the spiritual world. Everything else will follow from there.

Conclusion

A Message to the World

To some people, I say, look, you may have all these problems. Maybe you're crying over a divorce suit, losing your property, losing your children. You're devastated. You're down in the dumps. I'm telling you that there is something within your system that was given to you when you were born, and that's called the Spirit. And you must try your best to come to the realization that the Creator lives in that body of yours. You don't need to go outside of that. You go within yourself, and you apply peace to that spirit. Disconnect from all those woeful things that you're complaining about. Forget about them. Let them go. We are going to have to cope with those things, but during this intercession you have to come free with your spirit.

The energy might come in abundance. It's up to you. If you open up, it will come, and things will be really rosy.

But you have to maintain that. You can't go back to the negative habits that you entertained as you were growing up. You have to maintain that spirituality, and at the same time, you do your level best in coping with the circumstances that you have - the divorce, the children, the income, or whatever. This spirit is for all purposes. Some of the traditional people don't understand that. They say, "Our old ways are this...," and they fall right back into the dark shadows of negativity. You can only do your best at that moment.

Don't let anyone cause you to lose your perspective.

People often ask me, "How did you learn that? How are you capable of thinking that way?" All I can say is there are some innate gifts in certain people. The ancestors always prayed that this divine gift should never perish from the minds of the people. The Creator will always provide someone, even if it's someone not yet born, to benefit the rest of creation. The key is for the young people to realize this.

But you have to leave your ego out of it.

You must cultivate a keen sense of intelligence. There's no need to think everybody can do it. What's good for one is not necessarily good for another. Just like what cures one person doesn't cure all. Each affliction has to be matched with the personality in what is being used for doctoring, for example, for any plants being used. And the only thing you can use as a blanket cure is the Spirit. The Spirit is the only blanket answer to everything.

As long as we seek to identify as pure creations, to block out our identities, emotions, and other interferences, we become a link to the Spiritual Father, to the Spiritual Mother, and to the Spiritual Child - to the Creator in all his totality. That concept can free anyone.

In so many instances, so many problems, so many cases that I have been involved in, people have become very happy when they understood this. They came back to express words of appreciation because I have helped them through sickness, or through political or criminal activities. But I always say, "It's not me." I completely removed all of my personal attributes, like ego, anger, happiness - I have removed myself from that. I was able to be a true creation at the moment of crisis. It's as though I satisfied the spiritual process so that the Divine Power could come in and do its work.

That's the reason I tell people, "Don't lay it on me." Because it's not me, it's the Creator's work. If we were to take an assessment of how many people don't understand that concept, it would be devastating. From the top political figures in the nations, to everyone in the legal and judicial systems, it would be devastating to know how many people are still in the dark.

We could talk about the injustice in the justice department, and what they have done to so many people. Many innocent people are in prison, and it's not improving. When we think of what people are doing today that is in conflict with one another - the various religious factions and denominations; the republicans and the democrats; and right down to the Indian ceremonial grounds - who can rightly evaluate what they are doing? We have become a world of people who are following man's interpretation of the original spirituality.

They have lost sight of the universal concept that the Creator intended for people to have: To support one another. We might use some of the matrimonial concepts as teaching tools. What has happened to the words "for better or worse"? To support one another, no matter what affliction, no matter what sickness, no matter what mistakes have been made. This is the way we should regard our fellow humans, through the concept of a spiritual marriage to all creation.

One time, I went to St. Gregory's church in Shawnee, Oklahoma to talk about spirituality. At the end of the lecture, I opened it up for questions. This one monk who was sitting in the front row asked me, "How do we find our spirit?" I said, "The Spirit has already found you. You just want to be one with that spirit by eliminating all the distractions like your own ego; all the negative elements, anger, and other emotions. Free yourself from all the entanglements of today's world and abide by the spirit that's there within you. When you seek the Spirit, it finds you. It's already found you. It's been with you. You just need to know that." A lot of people in the audience were appalled that a monk would ask that. And here they thought he was spiritual.

There are all kinds of ceremonies out there that seek to give people a spiritual experience. Some even require a fee. And many of these so-called spiritual leaders are not right with themselves, with the Spirit. They watch one another; they are suspicious of one another - even within a church, even within a sweat lodge. In fact, the sweat was nothing more than to make the body strong and free from disease. It was a method for treating an ailment of some kind. It's turned into a temple - a temple of a false God. It's hard for people to understand that. And there's nothing we can do about it except practice our own belief in the Spirit.

Out west they have a lot of peyote sweat lodges. Some of those practitioners make up stories and tell people that others are inflicting negative things on you. It's really an unfortunate circumstance. They take part in turning family against family. A medicine man is supposed to tell the truth. The clients that believe him when he brings up negativity, for example, that your brother is doing this to you or your sister - it breaks up the family. I think on a larger scale, this type of division has been happening internationally.

Another time, I went to a conference sponsored by the Methodist Church. They invited many people like me all over the country to come and share our spirituality. What we had to say was very similar - our stories were conveying the same messages. We were there for one hour, and all of us decided there was an ulterior motive by the church people to get all of these stories for proselytizing purposes. We participated, but we didn't give out a lot of information.

Some of us went to sit under a shade tree, and these Onondaga Indians told me a story about a chosen one being born to a virgin girl. They have a story about an immaculate conception of a virgin girl from whom a child was born. It was very similar to the story of Jesus Christ in the Bible. He left them similar designs, the sacred squares of the wampum belts. We were talking about where these designs came from, and whether it was Jesus Christ who came to some of the tribes in this country. They wanted to know if my people had anything like that. I got to thinking, "I guess there was enough of my people that were still practicing the original rule of oneness, and that's why he didn't have to come and be born with us." Because through this oneness, you honor every God that has ever been. This is why many of our medicine prayers include Christ.

Many religions around the world tend to put all their eggs in one basket, in one object or another. Those objects don't mean a hill of beans if you've got the Spirit.

Some folks from India came to see me one day. They had given up the Hindu faith, and I guess they had been proselytized by Catholic missionaries. So, they were Catholics.

I said, "If you're willing to relinquish all indoctrinated concepts, including those of the Catholic Church and whatever you retain from your own cultural values, there's the chance that we can be blessed by Divine Power. You must lay them to rest during the moment that we do things, and only be you as an individual creation, knowing full well that God gave you a spirit. That's what we're going to use to join that spirit in full complement of what you are. We need to know how to retain the Spirit, and to quit racism, quit factionalism. To look at the whole world as one." I said, "If you're willing to do that, I'll venture to offer you some rituals. If not, that's OK - I'll still respect you." They wanted to do it, so I gave them a water treatment. They really understood what we were doing.

Our Keetoowah ancestors always tried to hold themselves in a humble manner. Few people today can maintain or master that humble and harmonious frame of mind throughout all activities and toward all people. So many people lose out to fanfare and a self-centered state of mind; they concentrate on their own ego.

Nevertheless, each person is given a choice: To maintain that which is spiritually right, or to choose to be away from that form of spirituality.

My grandfather, Redbird Smith, once remarked that although we remind our people time after time, some of them still choose to function in the darkness. But we have to continue to identify ourselves with the righteous spiritual existence that gives us intelligence and a positive outlook - that allows us to be industrious and to accumulate the essential needs of life. With this attitude, we can even accumulate beyond our needs so that we may share with others in need. The ones who are in need may be people who have themselves failed to comply with the spiritual concepts that everyone should be following.

Success by means of corruption or carelessly taking from the land destroys the true spiritual concept of a Creator-given way of life. When you look at what's happening today and what has happened by way of conquering other nations through war and deceitful maneuvering - those are not lasting concepts. Those misleading concepts will one day come to an end, which is why some of the most powerful nations have seen their downfall. From the Roman Empire to the various other historical empires, they have all failed.

Now, we are on the verge of the same thing repetitiously happening in our own country. The spiritual righteousness must encompass everything that we do each day of our lives. We have the resources to do right with every imaginable creation - plants, animals, water, land, air, each other. We must learn to stand as one with all nations, all people, all plants, all animals, inclusive of the ones who have gone before us, the ones living today, and the ones who have yet to come. In this concept, there is hope for us yet.

Smithy Ben Smith and Crosslin Smith

An Ode to my Brother

Smithy Ben Smith
1938-2018

On the hour of his passing - I didn't realize at the time - but after spiritually considering the conditions of our universe, I come to understand: the soft soothing rain, no wind, lightning, or thunder; the calmness of the conditions described Benny's life.

He is now a spirit. His spirit is as big as the universe, which describes the Keetoowah faith. He was a true Keetoowah.

Our grandfather, Redbird Smith, said "What we believe in and follow is the biggest thing, if we know how to become one with our spirit, mind, body and soul." Benny carried our grandfather's name, Totsuwa (Redbird).

We will always be one with Benny's spirit and with all things in this world, which means his teachings and his spirit are with you always, and he would want you to continue your life to the best of your abilities. It makes no difference who you may be in this world - you can be a Keetoowah or a true Christian - these are the ancient concepts to our ancestors from the beginning of human life.

Even after he's gone, the world will know about the true spirit. With love to all.

Crosslin Fields Smith

On the Crossing Over of

Elder Benny Smith

I was saddened to hear the news of Cherokee elder Smithy B. (Benny) Smith's passing on Saturday, September 22, 2018. He was 80 years old. The grandson of Red Bird and Lucy Fields Smith, Smith was educated by the Cherokee elders in the Cherokee ceremonial and spiritual customs. He completed his teaching certification in 1962 and received his Master's Degree in 1966.

Smith retired from Haskell Indian University in Lawrence, Kansas, in 2002 after thirty years of service, where he was assistant dean of students but often fulfilled other roles as a teacher, a coach, a mentor and a father figure to many students and staff. He was felt to be the spiritual foundation of the school, as well, sometimes leading memorials for students who had passed away and accompanying their bodies home to the family. He and his wife Cheryl regularly opened their homes to Native students who were homesick, giving them a meal and encouragement.

A gifted horseman, Smith's passion for training equines often landed him in feature stories in publications such as Western Horseman. His first name, Smithy, reflects his family's long involvement as farriers and Benny Smith was a fifth-generation horse shoer. He was a product of an Indian boarding school and noted that he arrived in a horse-drawn wagon and later sold one of his beloved horses to pay for college. Smith often said he considered his work with horses as therapeutic. He spent much of his retirement enjoying time with his horses and his family.

Smith was a first-language Cherokee speaker and although he lived outside of the Cherokee Nation, he remained close to his culture and family here, including brother Crosslin Smith. Benny Smith is credited with passing along many of our cultural teachings, including interpretations of the Cherokee clan system. He served on the board of the Cherokee Nation Education Corporation, and he often appeared at Cherokee Nation functions as a speaker and spiritual leader. He will be sorely missed.

Bill John Baker
Cherokee Nation Principal Chief

Crosslin Fields Smith

About

Crosslin Fields Smith

Crosslin Fields Smith was born November 27, 1929 to a traditional Keetoowah family. The members of the Keetoowah Society are best known as the keepers of God's Eternal Flame. Crosslin is a Korean War veteran, having served as a member of the famous 45th infantry, or "Thunderbird" Division of the U.S. Army. He holds a BS in Education and an Elementary & Secondary Teaching Certificate from Northeastern State University, and is now retired from a 30-year career of civil service.

Crosslin states that he has always represented the Cherokee Nation. He is the first employee of the Cherokee Nation - from 1964 to the present - as a spiritual resource person. He worked under Chiefs W.W. Keeler, Ross Swimmer, Wilma Mankiller, and the present Chief Bill John Baker. During the reorganization of the Cherokee Nation in the 1960s, Crosslin served as a U.S. liaison officer to his Cherokee people and was responsible for informing them on the status of negotiations between the tribe and the U.S. government. Through the years, he became the tribe's spiritual practitioner, performing blessings at official functions and at the start of new tribal development projects.

In 2014, Crosslin was among seven Cherokees honored at the AARP Oklahoma Indian Elder Honors event for their impact on their tribes and communities. A noted keynote and university lecturer, he has standing engagements in the United States and abroad. Crosslin states, "With the highest diplomatic credit and character, I have worked to build a Cherokee Nation for the Cherokee people. I fought in the Korean War. In this war, I represented the U.S. government and the American system. In all of my efforts, I worked to be part of the system instead of against it."

Crosslin and his wife Glenna live in Vian, Oklahoma, surrounded by their many children, grandchildren, and great-grandchildren.

Glenna Elizabeth Foster and Crosslin Fields Smith
on their 60th wedding anniversary.

About

Glenna Elizabeth Foster

Glenna Elizabeth Foster was born on September 19, 1929 in Sheep Springs, New Mexico on the Navajo Reservation. She grew up in the desert and mountains, farming and ranching with her family. She attended school and graduated from high school in 1950. She left the reservation to seek further education in Lawton, Oklahoma. In 1953, she completed the licensed practical nurse program, married Crosslin Fields Smith, and began practice at W.W. Hastings Hospital in Tahlequah, Oklahoma, where they settled and had five children. At Hastings, she assisted in the delivery of a multitude of Cherokee citizens while working in the obstetrics ward. Through the years, she worked the graveyard shift, raised a family, and accumulated 35 years of service to the Indian Health Service.

While Crosslin is an asset to the Cherokee community, he could not do it without Glenna. She supports and manages the finances and over-sees the food preparation and upkeep of the family home. She is also an excellent seamstress, craftswoman, and cook. She prefers to stay on the sidelines, lending support and letting her husband shine in his service and notoriety to the Cherokee Nation. For this, she received the 2018 Samuel Worcester Award from the Cherokee Nation, which is given to non-Cherokee individuals who have devoted their lives to the preservation of Cherokee heritage, culture, and sovereignty.

Crosslin and Glenna celebrated 64 years of marriage in August 2018.

Her five children are: Geraldine of Watts, OK, a graduate of the University of Oklahoma and a retired RN; Caroline of Porter, OK, a graduate of Northeastern State University and saleswoman; Crosslin, Jr. of Muldrow, OK, a retired Air Force serviceman of 20 years and currently Postmaster of Roland, OK; Catherine of Vian, OK, a graduate of Northeastern State University with a BA in Social Work; and Stokes of Vian, a graduate of the University of Utah with a Masters in Social Work.

About Crosslin Smith

Crosslin F. Smith is a man who has worn many distinct hats in his lifetime - veteran, educator, and spiritual leader. I am honored to call him my friend and mentor. He is one of our most important living treasures. He has always held a respected and emulated role in our traditional Cherokee community. His family taught him the old Cherokee ways, and he has practiced those ancient traditions as a medicine man and spiritual leader.

His door is always open for those who ask for help or need guidance. He is a member of the Keetoowah Society, which is known as the keepers of God's eternal flame. Crosslin has an unwavering determination to keep Cherokee culture alive and thriving.

Crosslin has the distinction of being the tribe's very first employee hired in 1964. He has worked under four Cherokee Nation Principal Chiefs - W.W. Keeler, Ross Swimmer, Wilma Mankiller and myself. His powerful voice, steady hand and spiritual ways are reassuring pillars of strength and comfort when he honors us with blessings at Cherokee Nation events.

He also has a special way to pay tribute to America's armed forces. During the Korean War, he represented the Cherokee Nation in combat as a member of the famous 45th Thunderbird Division, and he has performed blessing ceremonies for strategic and highly classified military operations over the past several years. That is not something many people know, but Crosslin is proud to provide it as needed and requested.

Hanging on to our old ways is challenging in a technology driven era. However, Crosslin has permanently protected our sacred traditions for future generations, and he has ensured these ways will never be forgotten. Times may change but history, culture and traditions do not and we have adapted to evolving situations, just as we always have as Cherokees.

Our survival as Cherokee people is knowing who we are and where we come from and Crosslin helps us remember these things. Throughout his life, he has helped countless people with his gifts. He has spent a lifetime representing our tribe and our values, and made significant contributions to Cherokee Nation and all of Indian Country.

The Great Spirit has blessed Crosslin with gifts, wisdom, kindness and a loving family. His role within the community, within the tribe is unquestioned. Without doubt, Crosslin Smith is a role model and treasure for our people. He has made it his mission to preserve our heritage. His work is from the heart, and it inspires all of us to do more for our fellow Cherokees and for all Native people. The people who know him and talk with him one-on-one are a living testament to his lasting legacy. I am proud of Crosslin, proud that he is my friend and proud of his accomplishments, including this book of insightful knowledge.

Bill John Baker
Cherokee Nation Principal Chief

Crosslin Smith is a wise and traditional Cherokee with a family lineage tying back to Redbird Smith. Crosslin is a confidant for many seeking traditional medical care. My family and I receive care from Crosslin and he is an invaluable part of our lives. In this day and age of the availability of highly technical and often complicated western medicine, it is comforting to know that a traditional medicine practitioner supports us with simple and natural ways that complement western medicine to prevent and heal any ailments that may come our way.

He is a keeper of healing knowledge that has been passed down through the generations of our Cherokee people. Each time I visit Crosslin, I learn something new that helps me better care for my family and myself. He has helped me to understand the Cherokee ways and to know what it means to be a Cherokee. My love and respect for Crosslin Smith are undying and I thank God he is a part of our lives.

Respectfully,
Julie A. Alvarez Erb, MPH
Cherokee Nation Citizen
LCDR, US Public Health Service
Epidemiologist, Indian Health Service

I recently had the pleasure of meeting and spending time with an extremely open, kind, non-judgmental, generous, gentle spiritual teacher, advisor, and friend named Crosslin Smith. Crosslin has the most open and clear eyes I have ever observed, and a vast amount of spiritual and traditional healing teachings. For the first time in my life all of the individual spiritual threads that have been sewn over time were brought together and woven into a beautiful, magnificent fabric. Words are inadequate and do not do this experience justice. Because words are all we have, I will do my best.

Crosslin understands the oneness and the connectivity of all in the universe. It is easy to say "we are all one," but to truly understand, grasp, and live this concept is another story. That is Crosslin's story. He understands the great mystery and the oneness of the universe. He comprehends that "we are one with him who is our source." If all beings understood this concept and united with The Source, then there would only be love, light, and forgiveness. These words are easy to write and difficult to live due to egos. Crosslin taught me that Creator's eyes are my eyes, and that I have a choice to follow Creator or ego. He communes with Creator and he is an enlightened, radiant being walking on mother earth in an earthly body as teacher for any who will listen.

Love, Light and Blessings,
Dr. Debbie Cunningham

You know how you know of someone by name or association of a group? This is how I knew Crosslin first. He is a Smith, and comes from the best-known family in Cherokee circles, real Cherokee circles. I met him in the late 1970s while working for the BIA, Tahlequah Agency. He became my boss. He and I worked in the Home Improvement Program (HIP).

One day, we heard the Cherokee Nation was going to contract (PL 93-638) the HIP program. The Nation staff started coming around and asking questions about the program and then asked if we would like to work for the Cherokee Nation. I had worked for them before but their benefits and pay was not good. But we needed jobs. We both became direct hires and began working for the Cherokee Nation. Wilma Mankiller was our supervisor. She had just been promoted from a grant writer to Community Development Director, which this was the job she got at the Nation when she came back from California. There is a project that Wilma asked us to help with; we were asked to work on the "Bell" project. We were the first ones to approach people of Bell and talk to them about what they may need. As it turned out the first thing people of Bell needed was Certificates of Degree of Indian Blood cards. You have to have these cards before you can get anything else from the government or the Cherokee Nation. I have always felt Wilma used us "Indians" to be the ones to approach the community. But this is another story.

Crosslin will tell a story of the day I lost an earring in his vehicle. But he puts a spin on the story that is not quite correct. He is good at that. He would seldom drive the GSA vehicle; instead he would rather drive his own vehicle, which had a dog box in the back. The dog box was for his coon dogs. He loved to hunt raccoons. And he always said that the Indian people we needed to visit would rather see a pick-up with a dog box in the back than a government vehicle. This is very true. Anyway, don't believe the whole story about my ear ring. We worked together for a few years. I was his secretary and he treated me more like an assistant and would teach me about every aspect of the HIP program. He would also talk about our people and what the old ones throughout time have taught our people. When he said "our people," I always take it to mean our ceremonial people.

This made me feel very comfortable, and I tried to learn as much as I could.

Not too long after working with the Nation, Crosslin decided to retire. He can relay the story of why if there is a story. After his retirement, we were still close, he often tells people I am his daughter. It makes me feel very honored that he feels this way about me. My trust in him just grew and grew; so much that when my children were little I always took them to him to be "doctored" before they started school every fall. Just for protection. They grew up knowing that they had protection from just the everyday evils of the world and now my daughter takes her children to him. He is a wonderful teacher and when he speaks to them, they listen. If it were not for Crosslin we, my family and I, would not know as much as we do about our ceremonies. Our leadership no longer teaches why we are who we are and what to do to survive everyday life. I am so grateful to have Crosslin in our lives.

Crosslin will from time to time tell me, "You should learn this. When I am gone you will need to do this." But I think, "I can't - I'm not worthy," because I probably know only a glimmer of what Crosslin has to do to protect himself and his family from what he must take on when he doctors people. A person like Crosslin sacrifices a lot to do what they do to help people. He listens to people and their problems, which is a burden in itself. He goes to get medicine and will be gone all day just finding the herbs and roots he needs for his work. And, not just anyone can find the medicine; my belief is it is truly a gift from the Creator to find the medicine and to be able to do all that he does to put what the Creator has given him to use for good. A chosen person like Crosslin must constantly protect himself and his family. I'm honored to be a part of his family.

I would like to talk a bit about our ceremonial grounds and the leadership. And I have been taught by Crosslin, that all this is happening and it has been told that it would happen by our old ones' teachings, but it doesn't help to know this and see what goes on there. First of all, we are like a lot of organizations that do things in the name of the Creator. Yet, because we are human beings, we do have shortcomings.

Our leadership a long time ago, when Crosslin's brother, William, was the leader started excluding Crosslin from any type of leadership activity. It has only gotten worse; he has been excluded from everything human there. He is not allowed to even lead songs during our dances. I remember a time when he was allowed to interpret what our leadership said during what we call "preaching" to those that cannot understand Cherokee. I used to sit with my family and listen to his interpretations and he did a great job. But even this was taken away. I suppose it is because they are human beings and they get jealous because Crosslin shares his knowledge of what is to be taught at the "grounds" and how things should be done. He will share stories that he was taught as a child by our leaders in that time, which are wonderful stories, most not written but they need to be heard. This heritage, tradition, teaching - whatever it should be called - belongs to all of us.

Crosslin teaches that our teaching, religion, what is ours should be shared with anyone who seeks to know. This is what the old ones taught. I think what we have as Cherokee people is beautiful and it is meant to be shared for all mankind that wants to know. Crosslin doesn't complain and says, "it's okay, they know it is wrong but they do this for themselves." I think Crosslin is brave for us, for those of us that can't do anything about what our leadership is doing to our ceremonial grounds.

I believe Crosslin may earn a special place in heaven for his work with people, all people, because he excludes no one.

Fan Robinson
Adopted daughter

My name is Melody McCoy, I am an enrolled member of the Cherokee Nation, and my clan is the Blue Clan (ani sahoni). I was asked to write about Crosslin Smith.

Most people know that Crosslin's father was Stokes Smith and that his grandfather was Redbird Smith. The Smiths are a very traditional Cherokee family. Some people are perhaps less aware that Crosslin's mother was a McCoy - Lilah McCoy - and the McCoys are another traditional Cherokee family. Lilah was one of twenty-two children of Alec (or Alex) McCoy, my great-grandfather. Another of Alec's children was George McCoy, who was my grandfather. George McCoy's son, also named George McCoy, is my father. So, my father and Crosslin are "half first cousins." Crosslin lives - and farms and raises cattle - on Alec McCoy's original allotments, in Sequoyah County, Oklahoma (Cherokee Nation District 3).

The land is beautiful. My Aunt Ahniwake used to say that when she visited "old Alec's land," she could still see the horse-pulled wagon that Alec had when she was a child bumping over the hills. On the land, where we still ride horses, hunt deer, and gather wild plants, the wagon ruts are still there, though now they're traversed by pickups, flat-bed trucks, and tractors. Portions of the land are quite timbered with area hardwoods like oak, hickory, and walnut. My Aunt once asked Crosslin how he deals with stress, and his response was, "I just go walk in the woods and talk to the Creator."

Crosslin is not just a farmer, rancher, and hunter. He is not just a brother, cousin, husband, uncle, father, grandfather, and great-grandfather. He is a prominent traditional healer among and for the Cherokee Nation. Crosslin has treated me and members of my family from time to time over the years, and I am well aware of the powers that he offers and with which he connects. Crosslin speaks Cherokee fluently, and he knows Cherokee traditions, culture, and wisdom. In 1999, Crosslin came to Boulder, Colorado to marry me and my husband in a traditional Cherokee ceremony. Fortunately, Boulder County includes American Indian tribal spiritual leaders as among the governmental and religious leaders that can officially perform such ceremonies.

Crosslin often is asked to speak at meetings, events, and gatherings around the country. He has done so at national, state, tribal, inter-tribal, and local occasions. He is an extremely effective speaker. Some years ago, he generously gave an invocation at an inter-tribal meeting that my office was co-hosting in Oklahoma. In attendance were many tribal leaders and Indian educators who regularly attend the frequent inter-tribal conferences nationwide. In that small meeting room in a large convention center, one tribal leader, who I believe was from the Pacific Northwest, remarked afterword that Crosslin had simply given the best native invocation that he had ever heard. I was filled with Cherokee pride.

But though he excels personally in public presentations, what strikes me the most about Crosslin is his unfailing day-to-day treatment of people - spiritually, medicinally, and literally. He genuinely understands, accepts, and respects that we all are true equals, without regard to race, age, gender, sexual orientation, ability, or disability. I know that he has treated people from around the world, he is known among indigenous communities world-wide, and he is contacted, if not visited, from people around the world. And these are just people - human beings. As Crosslin himself often says, "We (Cherokees) pray for all living beings and their eternal spirits."

Sincerely yours,
Melody L. McCoy
Attorney, Native American Rights Fund
Boulder, Colorado

I, Dr. Jody E. Noe, MS, ND, have known Mr. Crosslin F. Smith both personally and professionally for over thirty years. Initially in 1986, we met for the first time through a referral from mutual acquaintances in regards to an ethnobotanical research project I was undertaking as a part of my undergraduate studies. In 1987, Mr. Smith took me as a formal apprentice to study the Ethnobotany of the Cherokee and with this tutelage I went on to do a graduate degree (MS) in Botany with my research and thesis focused on my studies with Mr. Smith at Old Dominion University.

I have witnessed and experienced Mr. Smith through the years as a teacher, mentor, role model, and spiritual leader not only to myself but to all I have witnessed interacting with him. He was the High Priest Medicine Man of the Traditional Keetoowah for several decades until his retirement from this position, but has continued to practice his indigenous healing art daily with those who come to his home seeking help and advice. I have never seen him turn anyone away regardless of finances, race, gender, or religious beliefs.

I have witnessed Mr. Smith teaching to professionals, politicians, and the general public through the numerous conferences, gatherings and committees that he has participated in through the decades. He has been heralded as a Cherokee educator and highly sought after to participate as an educator at these assorted venues. When Mr. Smith begins to teach on any of his assorted topics of expertise, from education, Cherokee culture, to alternative medicine, he has the ability to speak in the vernacular of the target audience. With a commanding presence and wide breadth of knowledge, he is able to reach his audience at their level of understanding and bring enlightenment and a deeper concept of understanding to the lecture material.

Mr. Smith is not only a teacher and educator, but a spiritual leader and healer. He teaches in a conceptual manner integrating world religions and interdisciplinary faiths into the concepts of Cherokee spirituality. His teachings on spirituality can and have reached people globally as well as locally. Unlike many who teach on the practices of spirituality, Mr. Smith is unbiased, nondenominational, and teaches a real concept of interfaith amongst the religions of the world. Mr. Smith is a well-sought-after spiritual leader because of these attributes.

It has been my privilege, pleasure and honor to have been (and still am) a student of Mr. Smith. If it were not for his tutelage in all of these aforementioned areas, I would not be the doctor, researcher, and healer that I am today. Currently, we are working on an ethnobotanical academic research project through a research grant from my university, where I am a faculty - the University of Bridgeport College of Naturopathic Medicine. Through Mr. Smith's generosity in sharing his ethnobotanical knowledge, we are studying a native plant that he uses exclusively to help cancer patients. He will be published as a co-primary investigator with me once we have finished our academic findings.

Through Mr. Smith's selflessness and his ability to share his wealth of information to a wide variety of audiences, he has by "the power of one" changed the minds and lives of many. It is my great privilege to acknowledge this great man in my professional and personal growth as well as acknowledge all that he has done towards the "greater good" of all life on this planet, our Earth. May the Great Spirit always bless and keep him. Out of respect, humility and all humbleness, I offer this letter of acknowledgement for Mr. Crosslin F. Smith, my elder, teacher, role model, spiritual leader and friend.

Very truly yours,
Dr. Jody E. Noe

I first met Crosslin in the early 1980s. I have known him for roughly 30 years. Crosslin has been a mentor and inspiration to me and has been the father figure in my life. Crosslin told me that he considers me his son.

Crosslin has provided the inspiration behind the success of the National Indian Youth Leadership Project, by providing the cultural framework behind the positive approach that we have integrated into all our work, which spans twenty-five years or more. By understanding the power of positive thinking and how to frame everything we do in terms of the positive outcomes that we want to see with youth, we were able to develop a program that is recognized at the highest level of evidence based status that is attainable in the United States.

Project Venture is the only Native-developed program that has reached this level of recognition. Project Venture achieved Model Program status in 2005 and Evidence-Based status in 2007. This recognition comes from the Substance Abuse Mental Health Services Administration (Health and Human Services) and National Registry of Effective Programs and Practices. Crosslin has been providing prayer and ceremonies for protection for our camp program for twenty-eight years. In all that time, the most serious injury was a broken collarbone from a bicycle accident.

I have spent many hours in conversation with Crosslin, listening to explanations of how Cherokee medicine works, the principles behind it, and how Crosslin's personal spiritual connection helps him heal people. He has described how he was able to heal people from cancer, brain tumors and other assorted diseases and conditions.

Within my family, he helped clear away all traces of tuberculosis from my wife, after she received a positive TB test. He helped us when my wife went into labor with our daughter. Our oldest son required over twenty hours of labor, but when Crosslin went outside and offered prayer for our daughter's birth, she was born in forty-five minutes.

I have sent individuals with breast cancer to see Crosslin and they reported back that the next check up with their doctor revealed that the cancer was gone. I sent a friend who had MS to Crosslin and he began to follow Crosslin's instructions and reported back that his MRI was better than the one he had seven years prior. My daughter in law went to Crosslin for a diagnosed cancer and has been cancer free since he worked on her. There are numerous examples where he has helped me personally with various health issues.

One of the things I look forward to most in life is going to Crosslin's house and standing out on the porch of his log cabin and receiving a water treatment. I feel all the pressures of my life lifted away when I listen to the prayer and the songs and splash the water over my head. This is a ceremony that I do personally at every opportunity, when I have a stream or creek available. Water is the most powerful healer we have and I will pass this information along to my children and grandchildren.

Crosslin helped me to feel better about who I am, as a man who is not able to officially be enrolled in the Cherokee Nation, due to lack of paperwork. For whatever reason, my mother had no knowledge of written records of who her father or grandfather were. Crosslin understands that these people were Cherokees, but we don't know their names and can't make the connection to individuals who were registered on the Dawes Roll of 1907. My grandmother was born in Oklahoma Territory in 1905, with no record of the birth or the father. Crosslin has assured me over the years that my family has Cherokee ancestry and has accepted me. In spite of a birth certificate that states that my father is Indian, we understand that my mother's father and or grandfather is Cherokee.

Crosslin is a unique individual in so many ways. He practices what he professes. He is never judgmental and tries to find something positive in everyone he encounters. I have invited him to speak in various places, to offer the invocations at national conferences, introduced him to celebrities (Jane Goodall and others).

He spoke to over one hundred young Native participants at our annual leadership camp in 2009, in New Mexico. He was filmed as part of a documentary on Indian Health disparities at this camp. His presentation to the young people was so inspirational. He spoke about the original instructions, given by the Creator, to not only Indigenous people, but to all people. But he shared with the kids that our ancestors were instructed to be peaceful and non-violent and cooperate and respect all creation. He reminded these young people to harbor no negative thoughts toward anyone.

McClellan Hall

Reviews

Stand As One

In this work, Keetoowah/Cherokee elder and healer, Crosslin Fields Smith, shares his spiritually and ethically based vision of a moral and exemplary indigenous tribal heritage. His reflections are centered in the belief in a Creator whose original vision of human existence has often been distorted by human mistakes, foibles, selfishness, weaknesses, anger and misinterpretation.

Smith seeks to inspire his readers to achieve a spiritually based awareness of the need for a peaceful and responsible oneness with all of creation. In his narrative Smith features Jungian archetypes of renewal and peaceful coexistence as he encourages readers to achieve a benevolent Socratic ethical life commitment. He interprets human existence as a "journey of brothers who live with an open hand and open heart."

R. D. Theisz, Ph.D.
Black Hills State University
Proffessor Emeritus
English and American Studies

I have just read Crosslin Smith's book entitled *Stand As One: Spiritual Teachings of Keetoowah* and have found it to be full of wisdom, enlightening stories, truthful memories of tribal history and culture and stories of personal healing experiences. I thoroughly enjoyed his personal stories as well as the tribal history and knowledge he has passed on to us as his readers. I also learned much about the Cherokee people I didn't know. Having had personal experiences similar to his, I found his memoir to be authentically experienced and being shared truthfully. I recommend this book to be read by anyone including natives.

Howard P. Bad Hand
Ciçangu Lakota singer and ceremonial leader
Co-founder and intercessor for the
    High Star Sun Eagle Internatonal Sun Dance for Peace
Author of *Native American Healing: A Lakota Ceremony*

Given the current political vitriol and division in the United States, this country sorely needs a Crosslin Smith and his knowledge. Not only has Mr. Smith been a healer, a ceremonial leader and teacher but he is also a chief in the old tribal sense of the word. When his brother Benny passed away, I wrote a short note praising Benny as a true chief because he possessed the virtues of honesty, humility, generosity and courage. These qualities are equally those that Crosslin Smith lives every day of his life.

In his book, Stand as One, Smith outlines why and how the Keetoowah way is an important spiritual, philosophical and unifying message. More importantly, it describes what can best be called "native knowledge." As the late Vine Deloria, Jr., one of the foremost Native American scholars of the 21st century, explained in several books, numerous articles and speeches, Native or Indian knowledge is the understanding of human relations with the earth, the cosmos, the spirit world and with each other. It is the recognition that we all live in a complex world in which human beings, animals, plants, the spirits, the elements and even the planets and stars are tangible and interconnected so as to be inseparable. All things, in short, are living and are sacred.

Smith explains that the Keetoowah way is much more than a religion based strictly on ceremony but the connection of ritual with spiritual and physical well-being. It is the acknowledgement that a spirit is within each person and can be unified with the spirit of the creator of all things. The Keetoowah way is also the acceptance of the sacredness of the four great elements: earth, light or fire, water and the air. As Smith explains it, the Keetoowah knowledge also honors all of humankind. The ultimate unification of spiritual reawakening is the goal of the Keetoowah way.

Smith's book contains a number of implicit and profound lessons for our world. The first concerns modern leadership. It appears that on a worldwide scale, the tribal virtues of generosity, courage, humility and honesty have been replaced by cowardice, duplicity, greed and arrogance. If today's leaders would only adopt the virtues that Keetoowah spirituality emphasizes, a true human unification could be achieved. The Keetoowah way is, frankly, the opposite of the generally accepted Hobbesian idea that human beings by nature (or in spirit) are, and always have been, violent and egocentric. Empathy and altruism do not seem to fit into this idea of the human spirit. Crosslin Smith denies this view of humanity. The Keetoowah virtues are, in fact, based on compassion and collaboration.

Smith's knowledge also undermines the current use of the terms "tribe," "tribalism" and "tribal." In recent years, pundits, politicians and even scholars have redefined these terms to mean a group of humans united by hatred of others, a particular religion or sect, or a singular philosophy or worldview. These definitions apply more to the term "cult" than they do to "tribe." By definition "tribe" is a group of persons or clans descended from a common ancestor. Tribal governments range from democratic-republican-style councils to chieftaincies to gerontocracies. "Tribalism" can be many things but for the most part tribal people identify themselves not terms of "race" or color or physical morphology. They identify themselves with a place (territory, land), a particular history (oral tradition perhaps), a ceremonial cycle that usually relates to the changing seasons or to a part of the tribal historical narrative, the way members of a given tribe relate to one another and to a certain language that can be both liturgical and colloquial. Additionally, tribes were not exclusive of others; adoption of outsiders was frequent and tribal warfare was largely practiced taking captives in order to replace dead relatives and add to the population.

Keetoowah is the tribal way because it explains the ethos of the people so that a group can continue in harmony with the earth, the spirit world, the cosmos and each other. The Navajo call it Hozho; the Tohono O'odham call it Himdag. Each tribe has a word for it, and it means virtually the same thing: living in harmony and believing in the sacredness of all things. Mr. Smith's book unlocks the ethos of the Keetoowah way and provides an insightful look at Native American philosophies and spirituality.

Tom Holm, Ph.D.
Cherokee Nation Citizen
University of Arizona
Professor Emeritus
American Indian Studies

I have had two encounters with Crosslin Smith. In 1996, I needed traditionalist Cherokees for participants to enrich my dissertation. His wife said he was "out back on his tractor." She fetched him, and he spent 45 minutes advising me about places to go and people to talk to. A few years later, he came to my office in Okmulgee and spent almost an hour talking to me about ways of connecting to my clients and about some of the ideas contained in this book. Before he left, he took a tobacco leaf, dipped it in a jar of discolored water and flicked it at me and on objects in my counseling room. That night I dreamed of him looking into my eyes. His eyes are a peculiar color as I remember them, gray-green I think. They are eyes you will never forget once you have peered into them.

The book Stand as One: Spiritual Teachings of Keetoowah, is a short book that begins with an overview of crucial events of Crosslin's life as they relate to his spiritual journey. He interweaves traditional Keetoowah stories, specific healings he has conducted, critical historical events for Keetoowah people, philosophical and spiritual teachings that have existed from time immemorial and lastly offers a message to the world. Toward the end of the book, he also pays homage to persons who have profoundly impacted his life.

Early in the book, Crosslin tells his readers that not all people need the Keetoowah rituals that he shares with the world; in fact, many "spiritual people" may not need any rituals for healing. But most people do. Most people are not able to activate the resonant field of energy that exists within to bring about healing.

Crosslin is a medicine man who is part of a long evolution of healers who have learned ways of creating resonating spaces for clients where healing is available. He creates patterns of healing resonance with symbols and rituals that have been passed down to him. He tells us the spaces will change to some extent for each individual or group. He makes it clear that the healer must help the client to get outside the "normal" (as he says). The point of entry for this kind of healing is beyond causality. Symbols and rituals are languages of spirit that communicate to our deep subjective experiences. The client must be able to let go of objective reality and useful habit to be open to the resonant messages and wisdom available from their deepest spiritual self.

Crosslin tells us it is time for him to share Keetoowah wisdom and healing practices that have heretofore been held secret to all except Keetoowah people and, in many instances, held secret to all except Keetoowah Medicine people. In this review, I wish to discuss a few of the powerful lessons, I have absorbed from reading his words. He says that he began having "phenomenal experiences" in his early childhood in which he was freed from the "discordant physical world" and "pulled into a spiritual world that balanced body, mind, emotions and spirit. He says he would at first "go blank" and would at times hear "vibrations" that were communications from an "invisible world." He is teaching us about being open to Spirit. His mind becomes quiet and focused until he is in a heightened state that allows him to communicate with Spirit directly without egoistic thoughts intruding.

Later, in the context of healing, he says he cannot even rely on preconceived notions of healing in any given circumstance because every individual is different, and every circumstance has different variables to consider. To be a healer, one must be open to the Spirit, absorbing it and feeling its presence anew with each changing situation. To remain open to this dynamic requires extraordinary dedication. He says that a healer must "keep above negativity," maintain a positive attitude, and, ironically, "always know one's worth."

This last phrase is key to Keetoowah philosophy. "Knowing one's worth" is not a false pride. It is an awareness of who we are as human beings. The journey toward wisdom always begins with knowing that "Spirit is in your body, put there by the Creator." When Crosslin discusses Keetoowah principles, he again begins by saying, "You came from Spirit." And argues that all healing begins with "implanting" this "image" in persons who have "no good image of themselves." Spirit, the Creator, is embodied within us and is the focal point of spiritual opportunity and the prescription for healing.

Crosslin approaches healing with the question of who are we? He encourages us to know that there is no separation between the Creator Spirit and our individual embodied spirits. Any assumptions about who we are that do not take this into account block the fulfillment of our destinies.

Crosslin utilizes personal and ancient Keetoowah stories as spring boards for describing various "distortions and entanglements" that block our visions of health and wholeness and result in suffering and ultimately in illness. In one Keetoowah story a brother who is curious about why the sky is blue becomes increasingly greedy and self-interested while on his journey to the horizon and gets imprisoned in a realm between the spiritual and physical dimensions. Several stories describe how competitiveness leads from manipulation to negative attitudes which corrupt peace, beauty and any possibility of unitary awareness of the interconnection of all things in Creation.

Some of the most beautiful teachings propounded in this book are associated with the ancient Keetoowah Wampum Belts. The White Road Wampum Belt depicts stick figures on the purple edge holding hands, and hands reaching into the darkness for those who might want to take their helping hands. The Keetoowah philosophy teaches that there was once unity between human beings as well as unity with Nature. But because of the machinations described in the preceding paragraph, we became fragmented. The darkness that ensued has kept us from seeing the single spiritual connecting Force. But the darkness can be illuminated with our visionary minds when we realize the spiritual nature of reality.

Crosslin argues that human beings can lose the opaque, sick qualities of our beings in higher visionary states. Colossal energies are within us. Though too often imprisoned, they are waiting to be set free. Crosslin invokes his grandfather Redbird in bidding us to relinquish the doctrines of our churches that divide us, and to "give up all factionalism," including all deceitful maneuverings and false pride, none of which have any lasting value. He says that we should beware of compartmentalization, of imagining a schism between science and spirituality, or between reason and emotion. He invokes us to realize an epiphany of oneness which can only be achieved as we open inwardly to the Spiritual world. The realization of Spiritual nature is the end of religions and of all their doctrines. Crosslin is an advocate for the Universal Human Being, or as he advocates, "Stand as One."

Rockey Robbins, Ph.D.
University of Oklahoma
Professor

"If you want to achieve success in
whatever you set out to do,
you have to start as though you are
hand-in-hand with all of creation."
~ *Keetoowah Saying*

Made in the USA
Coppell, TX
07 April 2024

31016142R00052